The U.S. Navy at War

"Only the hits count!"

The U.S. Navy at War

Personal Accounts of 15 American Seamen,
Women & Marines During the First World War

Elaine Sterne

LEONAUR

The U.S. Navy at War
Personal Accounts of 15 American Seamen, Women & Marines
During the First World War
by Elaine Sterne

First published under the title
Over the Seas for Uncle Sam

Leonaur is an imprint of Oakpast Ltd

Copyright in this form © 2013 Oakpast Ltd

ISBN: 978-1-78282-092-5 (hardcover)
ISBN: 978-1-78282-093-2 (softcover)

http://www.leonaur.com

Publisher's Notes

Contents

To the Honourable Josephus Daniels
Secretary of the Navy,
whose devotion to the interests of the men in the
American Navy has been an inspiration to them
no less than to the nation as a whole.

"We're ready *now!*"—Navy slogan.

Jack Tar

We're not long on recitation,
We're just rough and ready gobs,
But we rate ten gadgets higher
Than some smug civilian snobs.
When we're out on well-earned shore leave
Drummin' up a little cheer,
Oh, we meet sleek city dandies
Who object to sailors here.
They are togged in pretty shirts
Like a lady on parade,
And they wouldn't touch a sailor
With a hoe or with a spade.
We may not be ornamental
In the tinselled dancing halls,
When the nation needs defenders
We are there when duty calls.
Though we can't hobnob with laggards
Who sleep in sheltered bed
And we can't enjoy peace pleasures,
We can join the hero dead.

The Wherefore of My Little Book

We have learned some things in war times that we did not know in days of peace. We have made the amazing discovery that our own fathers and brothers and husbands and lovers are potential heroes. We knew they were brave and strong and eager to defend us if need be. We knew that they went to work in the morning and returned at night just so that we might live in comfort; but we never dreamed that the day would come when we would see them marching off to war—a war that would take them far from their own shores. We never dreamed that, like the knights of old, they would ride away on a quest as holy as that of the Crusaders.

As for army and navy life—it had always been a sealed book to us, a realm into which one was born, a heritage that passed from father to son. We heard of life at the army post. We saw a uniform now and then, but not until our own men donned khaki and blue did we of the outside world learn of the traditions of the army and of the navy, which dated back to the days of our nation's birth.

We did not know that each regiment had its own glorious story of achievement—a story which all raw recruits were eager to live up to—a story of undaunted fighting in the very face of death that won for it its sobriquet.

Because the army lay at our very door, we came to know it better, to learn its proud lesson more swiftly, but little by little the navy, through the lips of our men, unlocked its traditions, tenderly fostered, which had fired its new sons to go forth and fight to the finish rather than yield an inch.

As a first lieutenant in the Girls' National Honour Guard, I was appointed in May, 1917, for active duty in hospital relief work. It was then that I came to know Miss Mary du Bose, Chief Nurse of the United States Naval Hospital, whose co-operation at every turn has helped this little volume to come into being.

The boys of the navy are her children. She watches over them with the brooding tenderness of a mother. Praise of their achievements she receives with flashing pride. With her entire heart and soul she is wrapped up in her work. Through her shines the spirit of the service—the tireless devotion to duty.

I had never before been inside a naval hospital. I had a vague idea that it would be a great machine, rather overcrowded, to be sure, in war times, but running on oiled hinges—completely soulless.

I found instead a huge building, which, in spite of its size, breathed a warm hominess. Its halls and wards are spotless. Through the great windows the sun pours in on the patients, as cheery a lot of boys as you would care to see.

There are always great clusters of flowers in the wards—bright spots of colour—there are always games spread out on the beds. There is always the rise of young voices—laughter—calls. And moving among the patients are the nurses—little white-clad figures with the red cross above their heart. Some of them appear frail and flower-like, some of them very young, but all impress one with their quiet strength and efficiency.

I have spoken to a great many of them. They are enthusiastic and eager. They praise highly the splendid work done abroad by their sisters, but they are serious about the work to be done here as well. Their tasks are carried on with no flaunting of banners, but they are in active service just the same, nursing our boys to health every hour of the day—giving sons back to their mothers—husbands to their wives.

It is a corps to be proud of and a great volume of credit should be laid at the feet of Mrs. Leneh Higbee, the national head of the Naval Nurse Corps. It was Mrs. Higbee who built up the corps—who has given her life's work to keeping up the standard of that organization—of making it a corps whose personnel and professional standing in efficiency cannot be surpassed in the world today.

As my visits to the hospital became more frequent, I began, bit by bit, to gather a story here and there, from the men who lay ill—stories of unconscious heroism—deeds they had performed as part of a day's work on the high seas.

They did not want praise for what they had done. They are an independent lot—our sailors—proud of their branch of service. "No drafted men in the navy," they tell you with a straightening of their shoulders.

And from the officers I learned of that deeper love—that worship of the sea—of the vessel placed in their hands to command. From them I heard for the first time of the value of a discipline iron-bound—rigid—a discipline that brooks no argument. There were stories of men who had hoped and dreamed all their lives of a certain cruise, only to find themselves transferred to the other end of the world. Did they utter a word of complaint? Not they! "Orders are orders"—that was enough for them!

And because those of us who send our men to sea are burning to know the tales they have to tell, I have made this little collection—the men's own stories, told in the ward to other round-eyed youths who gathered about the bed to hear, full of eager questions, prompting when the story moved too slowly.

What you read here are their stories—stories of whole-souled youths, with the sparkle of life in their eyes, with the love of adventure in their hearts. Jack Tar is an American clear through to his backbone!

Elaine Sterne.

New York,
May 15, 1918.

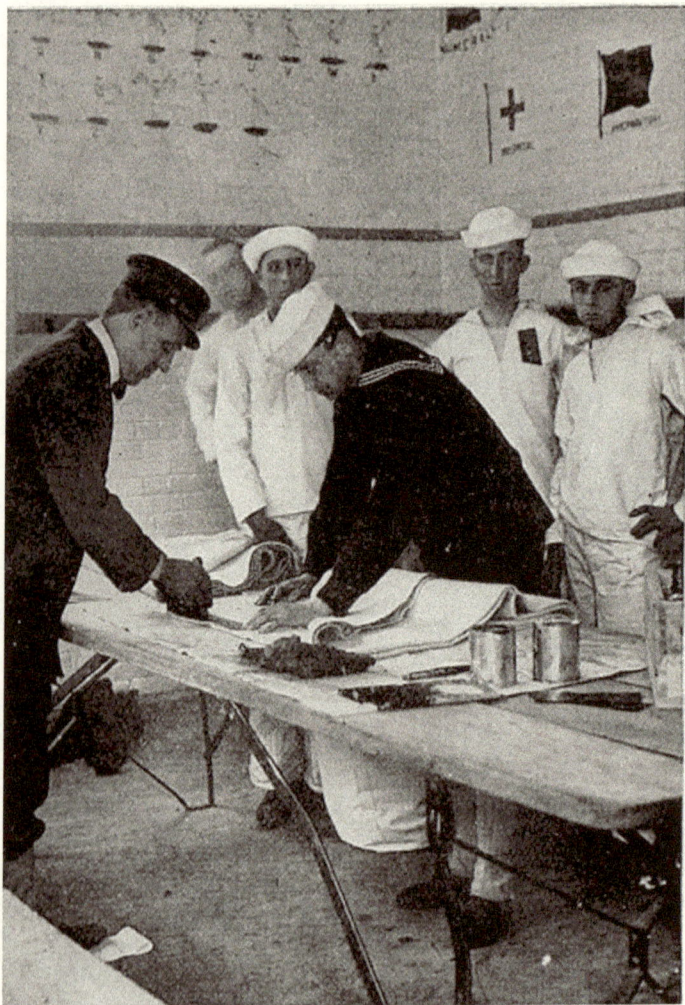

JACK IS HIS OWN "CHAMBERMAID."

Chief Gunner Blake Speaks

Somewhere along in January, 1915, I shipped on the U. S. S. *Utah.* Always had a hankering after the sea, and then, to tell the truth, civilian jobs were pretty hard to land in 1915—you bet they were!

Once you're in the navy you stay for a while. I liked it from the start. I got to know a thing or two about the guns, went to gunnery school; that's how I came to be made chief gunner's mate, I guess, and told to report for armed guard duty on May 29, 1917.

I drew an old tub. I suppose it had been used to carry a cargo of salt fish from Maine to Newfoundland, and here it was, painted fresh, and ready to cross the old Atlantic, which was fairly bristling with mines and lurking sea-devils.

We put to sea June 19th, and we reached the War Zone on July 3rd. I know what I'm doing, writing War Zone with capitals. You don't have to be told when you get there. You feel it in the air—it's like a wire vibrating; everyone's on edge, keyed up to G pitch.

It was my job to see that all lights were doused and all ports closed as soon as it got dark. I wasn't particular about the way I enforced orders just so I got them obeyed—and I saw to it that every man who carried a match was parted from it and that all pocket lights were put in a neat little pile—officers excepted, of course. They kept theirs.

Every hour I made a round of the ship, watching out sharp for a light. Important! Say, just suppose Fritz's sea-baby were lying off a few miles or so without the faintest idea that a merchantman, chuck-full of munitions, was a stone's throw away. Think how that German crew would feel if across the darkness they saw the flare of a match. Well, it would be apt to be lights out for us all that time—that's what.

The watch was doubled—four on and four off—a watch of good sixteen hours at a clip, with a life preserver on every minute of the time—that is, you were supposed to. On the transports the rule is carried out to the letter. Catch a man without a life belt and he can be pretty sure he'll be up for court-martial when he gets back to port.

But with us it was different. We kept them close by; some of the men slept in them. I had mine over my feet ready to snatch up in case of trouble.

It was July 3rd, remember, and we were feeling pretty good. My bunky was McCaffrey—Mac for short—a little red-headed, freckled Irishman from Wisconsin, the best that comes west of the Mississippi. We had it all fixed up to fire a gun off on the Fourth.

"Sure, it's a fine opinion Fritz'll have of us if he's thinkin' we're scared to let him know it's our big day back home," he argued.

I thought it was a great idea—I told him I'd stand by if he'd share the blame. Of course we knew darned well we'd never really pull it off, but it was good fun planning the whole thing just the same.

The sea was calm that night, for a wonder—just a gentle swell. We were on watch at eight, all on good lookout. Orders were to stand by, and the guns were primed, ready to shoot red hell into anything short of an ally.

I wish we could have had a close-up of us. Faces grim, tense from excitement, joking a bit under our breaths, wishing to Moses we could have a smoke, betting we'd get through without sighting anything better than our own reflection in the water.

Somehow we felt peppy. I guess it was thinking about the Fourth and what it stood for. Seemed queer to be in mid-ocean on the night before the Declaration of Independence was signed—yep, in the middle of a blooming black sea, with nothing in sight but a dash of white foam against your keel, where you cut along through a swell.

I'd just glanced at my radium watch and blessed the girl who gave it to me. It was nine. I glanced up. Not fifty yards away was a ribbon of white foam flung out on the water like a scarf, and, sticking straight out, by God, was the periscope of a German submarine.

No one waited for the command, "Fire when ready. . . ."

The ship was action electrified. I never saw a crew work like that. They fired point-blank and sent that periscope straight up to where all good periscopes go. Ripped her clean off.

We weren't sure we'd sunk her, but we figured we had. How did we feel? How do you think? That was celebrating the Fourth right and proper!

Mac, sweating like a horse, panting from excitement, managed to breeze by and chuckle.

"Didn't I tell you we'd shoot one off to show 'em who's who?"

It was a great night. We were heroes. We had knocked the stuffings out of a periscope; it stood to reason we'd sunk her.

We figured out how it happened. The submarine, when she was 'way out on the horizon line, must have seen us coming. She had evidently made a long detour, plotting our course and planning to arrive where she could take good aim and fire. What happened was that we changed our course, so that when she popped up she was plumb across our bow. Surprised! Wow! I bet her commander, if he's alive, hasn't closed his mouth yet!

It was something like this:

Well, we pretty well patted ourselves on the back, but German submarines must travel in pairs, like rattlesnakes, or else she came back to life, for an hour later she struck us amidships.

You know it when you're struck. Rather! The crash—the roar—the tremendous vibration—for a full minute, as the big hulk trembles and shudders—the hiss of water rushing into the boilers, the steam gushing, the sudden listing, and, worst of all, the throb of the engines silenced. . . .

You never forget that silence, felt rather than heard. It means you're a goner for fair. Above all the orders, rapped out like the clip of a hammer on steel—that noisy silence sounds loudest in your ears.

"Stand by your guns. . . ." Sure we did. While there was still a chance we wanted to get a whack at that sub., but all the time I was worrying about Mac. He was taking a watch off. Could I reach him?

". . . Get back, you damned fools. . . ."

". . . Man the life-boats!"

". . . Gee, that's a close one! Look spry or you'll wash overboard. ."

We didn't leave our post until the last life-boat swung clear and landed with her crew. A couple of boats had been smashed against the side of the ship and we heard the yells of their crew—nasty sound, that.

I forgot about my life-belt—I wanted to find Mac. I couldn't. It was pitch black. The water was waist deep and washing over you in gigantic waves. There was only one chance—to jump for it. I took it. I landed near the propellers. I could hear them churning fiercely—I could feel their suction drawing me to them. I guess I fought like a fiend. I'd heard about the death men die drawn into that blasted hole the ship makes when she goes down to Davy Jones.

I didn't think of home. I didn't think of my past sins. I just thought with every ounce of my strength that if I could keep swimming for a few seconds more I could be clear of that undertow. I made it.

All around me men were calling for help. I made out a life-boat a few yards away and hollered to them, and just then an oar floated by.

I never was so glad to see anything in my life. I rested on it and caught another. Two oars! Why, it was as good as a raft. I was safe—if only I could find McCaffrey in that black hell.

I yelled his name and heard a sputter behind me.

"For God's sake, save me———"

"Can't you swim?"

"No."

"Stay where you are; I'll get you."

It was Spick, one of the oilers—a big chap, weighing a good one-ninety.

"Steady! I'm coming."

He grabbed the oar and lay across it, a dead weight. Someone else pulled me down.

"Help!"

It was little Tucker, mess attendant, a kid of seventeen. He was all in. I shoved them both along, and they were heavy, let me tell you. Someone in the boat saw us and drew alongside. They lifted us in.

"Where's McCaffrey?" I asked them.

Just then I saw him. He was swimming straight for us. I let out a yell, but it died in my throat.

Straight out of the water, not twenty yards away, rose the gray bulk of the submarine, its greenish light casting a weird glow over that awful scene of struggling men. Fritz's war-baby had come back to gloat over the damage it had done.

Our captain, with his pocket light, was flashing the Morse code on

16

the water as he floundered about.

From the deck of the submarine the commander's voice rang out. He spoke as good English as I do.

"What ship have I hit?"

Someone told him.

"Where is your captain?"

Silence.

"*Where is your captain?*"

Then it was that little Tucker, sitting forward, tense, leaned far out and yelled:

"Douse yer glim, Cap, douse yer glim. . . ."

Out it went. The commander gave an order. We couldn't hear it, but we were afraid he meant to make straight for us and cut us in two. We pulled away, but, instead, he was wishing us the best of luck to lie there and rot, and then they submerged—just vanished into the black water from which they had appeared.

We waited trembling, but nothing happened. There wasn't a boat in sight. The old hulk of our ship had gone down forever. I thought of the captain and of McCaffrey.

"Let's get 'em now, mates," I urged. But from the direction in which we'd last heard them there came no sound. They weren't there. Nobody was. So we pulled away.

It was a leaky boat and we stripped off our shirts—anything we had on that was white, so that in case Fritz came back he could not sight us. We needed the shirts, all right, to stuff up the holes in the boat. Those who weren't stopping up the holes took turns bailing. We bailed like fiends—no time to think—no time for anything but to hope a convoy would pick us up.

Along toward dawn, at six-thirty to be exact, our own convoy sighted us. The boys were pretty stiff from exposure, but I was all right—all right and fighting mad—my matey had gone down.

"I'll *get* that *Kaiser*," I told them. And I will, too. That's why I'm shipping on a destroyer next. I'll get that *Kaiser*, see if I don't.

17

The navy's first capture—German submarine, U-58, surrenders to destroyer "Fanning."

Chief Petty Officer Wilson Speaks

WAR CLOUDS GATHER

The French are a whole lot different from us—more easy-going-like. They make their money and spend it free. I like that about them. Not like some people I know who won't let go of a nickel once they gets a death grip on it.

Well, say, when we was anchored at Villefranche we come to know a thing or two about the Frenchies. Villefranche is just over the hill from Nice—a nice jaunt of a couple of miles or so, or if you've a mind to, you can take a little car that gets you there before you know it.

Nice is on the style of Atlantic City. If you ask me, I like Atlantic City better, but then that's because they speak United States there. Still Nice has a great bathing beach—you have to hand it to them—and you get so you like them little tables set out in front of the *cafés*, where they "*parlez-vous*" with each other and drink quarts of red ink.

We'd hike over to Nice every shore leave. Some of the crew went as far as Monte Carlo, but not me. I was satisfied. Besides, one place was as sporty as the other, if that was what you wanted. They was chuck-full of what the French call the "*joie de vie*," which in Yankee means "plenty of pep"—that's it.

You always felt happy there and the people was great! Didn't seem to take nothing serious—the Frenchies don't, in peace times. The women had a twinkle in their eye and a kind of sparkle about them, and the men said pretty things and twirled their canes—oh, they was a cheerful lot, all right.

Remember, all this was before the war. It was August. Hot. Still. Can't you see it? The sea, where our boat lay at anchor, calm as glass and blue as a turquoise. The sand along the beach, snow white.

It was a Saturday, and we had a forty-eight, which took us ashore at ten in the morning. Didn't want to miss no time on land. The day

19

was so fine that we decided to foot it into town. Everything was green and growing and smelled good. We took our time and ambled into Nice long about chow. The minute we hit that port I knew for sure something was up.

Oh, don't think there hadn't been war talk flying about. Sure there had, but, except for a general uneasiness, you wouldn't know nothing was doing. The Frenchies are like that—they don't hunt trouble, but when it comes—oh, boy! They sure are right *there!*

We seen little groups of folks standing talking together. The shop keepers had left their shops, and joined the crowds on the street. They was waving their hands—they are great on that—everyone speaking at once. We come up close and listened. What we heard certainly made our ears ring!

War! France was going to declare war on Germany! Queer how that black cloud seemed to change the whole complexion of that little sun-soaked town. I'd never seen the natives look like that before. There was a little old woman who kept a fruit stand—figs and peaches and what-not. She always had a grin for us fellows when we passed. She and her granddaughter. The granddaughter was a pretty girl—her cheeks was as red as the side of the peaches and she had black eyes and hair. They was always ready to swap a *"bon jour"* with us—but not today. The old lady was minding the stand alone. She looked kind of white—no smile—no wave of her hand. She told me her grand-daughter had gone to the square where the bulletins was being posted. We beat it over.

It was about three; no, I guess it was four, before the big crowds began to gather in the square. Up to that time there had been little groups drifting here and there, but by four the wagons had stopped at the corners, their drivers had climbed down from the seats and pushed their way into the mob, and the tram-car conductors and motormen just left their cars wherever they happened to shut off power, and shoved their way in for a view of the bulletins.

I tell you, that little town was at fever heat! Excitement! Say, nothing beats a Frenchie at that! I've seen a lot of things in my time, but it certainly gave me a queer feeling in the pit of my stomach to realize just what those bulletins meant. It kind of got you to see that little pleasure city so dead serious all at once.

Everyone in Nice was in that crowd—rich man, poor man, beggar man, thief. The ladies from the Riviera, in their silks and satins—the tradespeople—the poor—all fighting for a view of the words flashed on the boards.

Someone yelled, "*Vive la France! Vive la France!*" and a thousand voices caught it up until it rose and swelled like the roar of the combers in a storm.

We had seen Nice quiet and peaceful and pretty—we saw a different Nice from that moment. They didn't waste no time. They began calling in the reserves. Do you know how they done it? Why, they'd simply gather them up as they went along the street. From buildings and shops and hotels and huts they poured—boys for the most part—some pulling on a coat and buttoning it as they ran, and women following them, always women—sweethearts and mothers—looking puzzled and dazed by it all, but never holding the boys back—not they!

I never seen fellows mustered in that quick. The streets were choked with men—sharp orders rang out, and the blare of trumpets and rolling of drums. Say, I had to pinch myself to be sure I wasn't dreaming it! You read about such things, but you never expect to see them with your own two eyes!

Some few men had uniforms or parts of uniforms. Some carried old swords their fathers had fought with before them. Some of them sang as they marched to their barracks, arm in arm. Some broke away and ran ahead, calling to a pal, stopping to speak with an old friend. And always, lined up on either side of the street, was the raving, crazy mob that cheered them, flinging up their hats and waving handkerchiefs.

Outside the *cafés*, at the little tables, wine was flowing like water. One glass after another flung down with a toast to France. They didn't stop at that. I seen a little girl spring up on a table and hold her glass high; all the folks at nearby tables jumped to their feet, cheering her. I couldn't hear what she said, but suddenly she straightened up and began singing the "*Marseillaise.*" Lord! The whole town caught up the tune—it came from everywhere. Women in open windows above the street, leaning way out over the sills, sang it; children in the street piped up; there wasn't no one too young or too old to join in.

The boys marching by grinned at her as they shouted it, and she waved to them.

At a crossing I caught sight of our little old woman. She was shelling out all the fruit on her stand to the boys as they passed. The tears was rolling down her cheeks, but she smiled at them just the same.

I didn't see her granddaughter until sometime later; then I found her with a fellow who was dragging on his uniform coat and talking to her at the same time. She helped him fasten it, her eyes on his face. I never seen anyone look so hard at a man—as if she could eat him up with her eyes. When he left her she stood staring after him. I wormed my way in through the crowd until I got alongside of her and I took her arm, but she didn't seem to know I was there.

Bulletins was flashed every few minutes. No sooner would one get posted up than they would tear it down to make room for another. Above the roar of voices rang out the call to arms, and always from no place in particular men and men and men came pouring, keen to get into the Big Scrap.

You couldn't take a train if you wanted to. Everything was commandeered for the "military," as they call it over there.

The sun went down and the street lamps began to wink at you and still the excitement raged. Bulletins—crowds—trumpets—voices—soldiers arriving from Monte Carlo and a new set of cheers for them. No sleep for nobody, just moving through the packed streets listening to a snatch of conversation here and a snatch there.

And every passenger coach and freight train jammed with soldiers on their way to the concentration camp. Those who had any, wore the old French uniform—you know, the red pants and blue coats—great colours, but say, what cruel targets for Boche bullets they turned out to be!

Next day the cry went up for horses—they needed horses, and they got them. That's the Frenchies' spirit for you. Nothing is too much to do for their beloved country. Every farmer with a four-legged animal drove into Nice and gave him up gladly, and what's more brought in all his garden produce for the boys.

It was like a horse mart. I never seen so many sweating, rearing, stamping brutes. One farmer drove in a little blind mare he'd raised from a colt. Rummiest horse I ever seen. Wind-broke, with a coat that looked like the moths got into it. The old man seemed pretty fond of her, for he talked to her considerable before he parted from her. He didn't pay no attention to the crowd looking on, only he just kept whispering in her ear and stroking her nose. After a while he turned her over to the officer in charge.

"I have explained to my friend that she must fight for France and she has said in that case she is willing to go," he told them in French. They took her, too, and he hiked back a dozen miles or so without another word.

22

Once on the ship again, we laid in the harbour at Villefranche for a week, but from the deck you could see the little seaport town and that line of men that wound over the hill—tramping—tramping toward the sunset—thousands of them—an endless stream.

We went to Gibralter. Just to let you know how particular them British ships had become let me tell you that they halted us at sea one night and made us run up our colours. They weren't taking no chances.

We laid there another week—no liberty—nothing. We knew then we was in the War Zone. The gates were down and only the French and English allowed in. You couldn't even coal your ship, and what was more, we were in direct line of fire from the British guns behind us. We heaved a sigh as we started down to Tangiers, Morocco.

Some contrast! No excitement—no faintest hint of a war. Just a dirty Arab town with streets so narrow your shoulders graze the walls on either side. Dirt and flies and beggars.

We was burning up for news—we went crazy tied up there a month. Then we went home and learned what was happening. We heard about Verdun and the Kaiser promising to make Paris by Christmas and all such rot.

Folks asked us what we thought of the war. I used to say, "If you want to know *my* opinion, I think the sooner we lend those Frenchies a hand the better!" and that's just what we're doing—at last!

You get so you love them if you stay around them awhile. They're so happy and cheerful, but when there's business to be done you can't put nothing over on them! I won't never forget that old fellow and his blind mare. Gee! How he did hate to part from her! But that didn't stop him from doing it. But then that's Frenchies for you—nothing is too much. . . !

"General Byng"—Friend and mascot
of the U.S.S. "Recruit."

Commander Woodman Speaks

The Stuff Heroes are Made of

Honour Medal for U. S. Sailor

First Award Goes to Ohio Man Who Saved Balloon Pilot

Washington, Nov. 12.—The first naval medal of honour award
ed during the present war was announced by Secretary Daniels
today as the reward of Dennis O'Hara, who rescued the pilot
of a kite balloon which was struck by a squall in the submarine
zone.

The balloon was being used for observation purposes by a
United States cruiser. The pilot was saved by O'Hara from the
submerged basket of the balloon.

When is a hero not a hero? Do you know, if there is any one thing
this war has proved to all of us, it is the fact that every man jack of
us has a large and totally unsuspected slice of courage tucked away
within him somewhere. We never used to think so. We used to suppose that the ability to be brave in the face of death was a great gift
granted only to a chosen few.

Do you remember wondering how such heroes came to be born
as the men of the "Light Brigade," who rode without a quiver straight
into the jaws of hell? We read in our history books of Perry and Far-
ragut, or we heard the veterans of the battles of Lake Erie and Mobile
Bay tell the stirring tales. I used to suspect that these men, whose
names went ringing down the halls of time, were of different stuff
somehow—a sort of super-calibre—I never thought to see the day
when the greatest deeds of fearlessness, of self-sacrifice, would be performed on the field of honour by the butchers and bakers and candle-
stick-makers of this country.

Take a clerk who has toiled at his desk for ten long years. He is afraid of death because he has time to be, but close up his books and dry his pen and let him join the army or navy—build him up—make his white blood red and send him on a destroyer or order him over the top—afraid of death! not much he isn't!—too intent on launching a depth charge or sniping a Hun to think about it.

Besides, once you get used to the idea that every minute may be your last you don't seem to mind it. You rather relax and you don't worry; you obey orders and stand by—and you are determined to be as game as the next fellow when the Great Call comes.

Heroism is a large word for all this. It is just a part of the day's work. That's what I like best about the youngsters in this war who have done deeds of bravery that can stand up beside any acts performed in the days gone by. They are indignant if you praise them. Yes, they are. They tell you impatiently that what they have done anyone else would do. Perhaps it is true. I guess so. But you have to let it go at that. They won't stand your making much of them. Not by a long shot.

Take the case of the boy on our ship. He was a capable chap, who went about his duties without attracting a bit of attention. Just one of those splendid cogs in the war machine—a Chief Petty Officer, who wasn't looking for glory or honour medals, but was just doing his job to the best of his ability.

Our trip over had been without thrills, unless you work up one on your own by wondering how it happens with the number of ships at sea minus a light there are so very few collisions. That always interested me. I remember one black night when we were shipping seas over the fo'ca'sle that were sending sprays to the bridge. The darkness hung about us like a velvet curtain. As far as we knew we were the one and only bark afloat on the whole Atlantic, and yet when dawn broke, we sighted a convoy going east. If it hadn't been for pure Yankee luck she might have been in the same latitude as we were. Had the meeting come a few hours earlier or our course been a trifle different the results might never have been told.

But that is side-stepping my story, isn't it? We had an observation balloon attached to our ship, which we flew with considerable success during the first part of the voyage. We were nearing the point where we expected to join the vessels sent out from France to meet us, and as the captain wanted the balloon to be aloft that morning, she was sent up a good bit earlier than usual.

It was a squally, rainy morning—the sort you expect in the North Atlantic. The sea was rough, and I suppose we were making about thirteen and a half knots. There was considerable wind on our starboard bow.

In the balloon basket was a young officer. He understood managing the big bag, so we sent him up about a thousand feet. We passed through a rain squall and the balloon rode that tip-top. He telephoned to the officers below that he'd like to stay up for a while as the wind seemed to be dropping.

About a half-hour later we entered another rain squall. It was a nipping cold one—far colder than the first. The combination of chilled rain and strong wind was too much for the balloon. First thing we knew the bag had crumpled up like a crushed-in derby. And, before you could say "Jack Robinson," down she flashed like a shot, her buoyancy gone, and the little basket suspended about fifty feet below her, riding the crest of the big waves like a tub.

Inside the basket, busy as the busiest bee that ever came out of a hive, was that young officer, throwing out ballast as fast as the good Lord and his right arm would let him.

It had the desired effect. Up rose the balloon, until it climbed to about five hundred feet, but with its ballast gone it was like a kite without a tail—a wild balloon at the mercy of the wind. That was a sight you did not soon forget! All hands were on deck staring up with bated breath—a few tried to shout advice, but the gale drowned out their voices and the boy in the basket was far too busy hanging on for his life to heed us.

The facts of the case were that he was virtually a prisoner, with the ropes so twisted about the basket, as it swung on high in its fantastic dance of death, that he could not have saved himself if he would. We didn't get onto that at first. We rather expected to see him shoot like a projectile through the air. It certainly seemed to us that he must be the one exception to the law of gravitation, for by all rights he should have been hurled earthward at least a hundred times by that careening, dipping kite. And as it swung and lunged and turned over on itself in wild contortions it reminded me of a mad beast tugging frantically at its leash to be free.

There was only one chance of saving him and that chance was a small one against the almost certain sacrifice of many lives. To stop the ship was the one chance, but a ship with engines dead in the war zone is a first-class target for the subs, and I can tell you that any man with the responsibility of hundreds of lives on his shoulders is loathe to give the order. But the sight of that pitching, rearing devil, with its fragile cargo—one human life—was a sight no man could well resist, and the captain finally gave the order to slow down.

We went aft. The balloon hung over our port quarter, and, as we drew it toward the ship, we got hold of a trailing line from the nose of the bag. The big kite came docilely enough, as though it were tired of the game it had been playing and was sorry for the damage it had done. But the basket, with the man inside, was in the water, half submerged and in great danger of going down before help could possibly reach him.

Now here is where the hero part of the story comes in. It was so quietly done that we did not know, until we saw a man flash over the side of the ship and down one of the basket lines, that a rescue was being attempted.

The ship still had headway and the sea was running high, neither of which argued well for any chap trying to save a human being caught fast in a maze of rope.

The basket was three-quarters submerged. The boy inside was played out and could offer no help, but the C. P. O., clinging fast to his bobbing goal, went to work with his knife and a singleness of purpose that no mere raging sea could shake. He hacked away at the imprisoning ropes, his teeth clenched, and at last crawled into the basket and got a bowline under the officer's shoulders. We hoisted him aboard, and while we were doing it, the C. P. O. clambered up to the rail, where eager hands drew him over.

But he did not want our praise. It embarrassed him. What he wanted most of all was to get into dry clothes and to go about his duties. Hero! He grinned at the word. Just the same, that is what he was—a real American boy with steady nerves and quick eye and plenty of pluck. Oh, yes, there are lots of heroes at large these days, but they do hate like the very dickens to have you call them that to their face.

Chief Yeoman Lang Speaks

Depth Bombs and Destroyers

Eight years is a long time in the service. But it pays. Yep. Even if I never draw a commission I'll get a pension of one-third my full pay after another eight years, and if I stay in for thirty years, all told, I'll pull down over a hundred dollars a month for the rest of my days—me— just a chief yeoman. Now, that's not bad, is it?

I've seen quite some service. You know about that little party at Vera Cruz last year? I was right there in the front row. I've always been ready for a scrap provided they gave me destroyer duty. Nothing else goes with me. Once you get used to the feel of that rolling deck under your feet you can't be happy on any other bark afloat!

There is nothing speedier or lighter on the high seas. She will ride the waves like a bottle that's corked up. Not following the trough of the swell like a man o' war, but bobbing right over the white caps or burying her nose deep in the water as she cuts through.

. . . And spray! Say! If it wasn't for the shield around the fo'c'stle-gun, you'd swim to Europe. As it is the combers sweep the deck in rough weather like a young Niagara. High boots help you some, but the only way to guarantee keeping a good man aboard is to lash him to the gun.

There is a temporary shelter for the gun crew in the pilot house, but say, when the waves get too sassy the gunners aren't ashamed to rig up a line which they hold on to pretty tight let me tell you, as they stand by.

Greatest sport in the world to have an ice-cold spray breaking over your deck. Yes, and freezing so hard you have to take a hatchet and chop it. You never are entirely dry, and you're never sure each minute won't be your last. But, say, you wouldn't change places with a commander on the biggest warship afloat!

Queer, how you come to love the bobbing little devil. I guess it's human nature. The more cantankerous a proposition is the more you like to handle it. And salt water doesn't hurt you any. Good for you. Don't they give you salt baths and charge you a stiff price? Well, we get the treatment free. Pretty soft, I call it.

We had a great crew. I was chief yeoman, with a job of clerk, and in time of action I had to work the range-finder. I was pretty busy, but I did have time to ring in a few laughs at the ship's pet. He was a Swede—Ole Hjalmar, and big! Say, he was eight feet high—or, anyway, six-two, with a voice like a bull. He was mostly ears, and he had blond hair and high cheek bones. His face was red from the high winds. It browns mine, but it made him look like a ripe tomato.

He hated his pink cheeks. We used to guy him about them, but most of all we made fun of the big gold rings in his ears, and say, I don't think there was a square inch of him that wasn't tattooed—stars and pigs and anchors and eagles all over him!

Education didn't bother him any. The only writing he did in the twenty years' service was to sign his name to his pay checks. But he was always ready with a laugh. He was boatswain's mate and his job was official scrubwoman and then when an officer gave command he had to pass the word.

I remember one day we were expecting to make port that afternoon. It was wash-day and as we changed our course it happened that the clothes we had hung out in the sun to dry found themselves in the shade. Our bags were still wet, so Ole was told to pass the word to the men to shift their clothes to the other side of the ship.

"Aye, aye, sir," boomed Ole's big bass,—then he gave the command.

"All you men who iss got clothes ver de sun isn't iss, put 'em ver de sun iss iss. . . ."

Say, that got us! and Ole never did hear the end of "ver de sun iss iss." That was all right, as it turned out, but next time—well, this is what happened.

We anchored in an English port and like every good "bloomin' bloody Yank," as our British cousins call us, we got out our bats and balls ready to play United States baseball. We had four cracking good teams on the ship. The first and fourth would play, then the second and third. The competition was pretty close and we were tickled to death when the American Consul got a tract of land for us and we went ashore to show those Johnnies a regular game, after watching

30

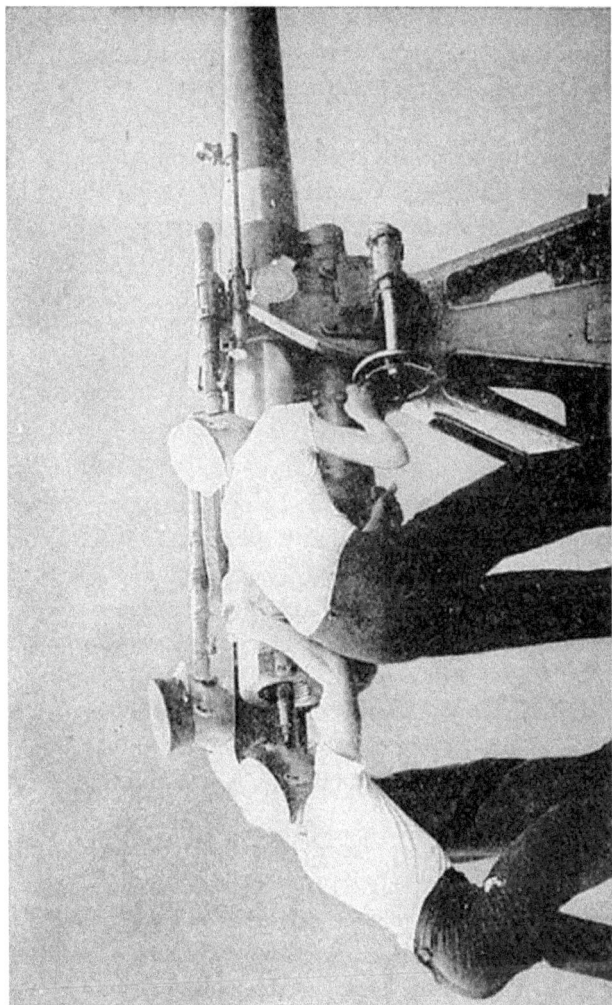

"Boresighting"—A 3-inch gun on board a merchant ship.

cricket for an hour or two.

Well, after several days of games, some of the men began abusing their shore privileges, and the officers knocked it off and kept us aboard—no liberty at all!

Gee, we certainly longed to get off the boat. There was land only a hand's throw away—and there was a whole diamond going to waste and games tied. One afternoon, after talking the matter over, we plucked up courage and drew lots. It fell on me to go up to the Officer of the Deck and ask for a Recreation Party.

I did.

He didn't waste any breath at all. "No," he said, so I slunk back to my mates. But we didn't let the matter rest. Every ten minutes another one of us would march up with the same request. The O. D. got sore. Ole was on watch.

"Pass the word," the O. D. commanded crisply, "*No Recreation Party whatsoever!*"

Ole did.

"*No Recreation Party what's er matter?*" he hollered.

That finished him. He lost a rank on account of it. Poor Ole, he got in dutch for fair!

We were convoying merchant and troop ships, going out to meet them and bringing them back to port. We started out one cold October day with a raging gale blowing. The sea was like a seething caldron—the waves were mountain high. We had on all the warm things we owned, but, at that, we were ice wherever the water struck us.

I was muffled to the eyes. Esquimos had nothing on me and I could see we were in for some stiff duty. It wasn't a matter of one day—it was a matter of eight days on a raging sea—no chance to take off your socks even—life-preservers on every minute of the time—watching out sharp for Fritz.

A flock of us met the ships we were to bring in and we started to steam back to our base, when we had the shock of our lives!

It was early morning, barely light. The sky was a gray line, as if you took a paint brush and slapped a streak from east to west. The water was gray and we men on the bridge rubbed our eyes, for right in front of us, not five hundred away—standing out black against the sky—was a German submarine.

We figured she had laid there all night—and was going to send our flagship to the bottom if she could—but she couldn't have looked over her shoulder, because she didn't seem to know we were there.

32

Well, we were after her like a streak of greased lightning. That was just what we had been praying for; as we charged her we fired; we were almost on top of her, trying to ram her, when she submerged; we passed right over her as she went down; you could see the bubbles and spray.

Then we launched our depth charges—"ash cans," as we call them. They look like a ten-gallon drum. You set them off when you are travelling full speed right above your blooming submarine—fifteen knots we were making.

Quick! Say, it's the speediest work in the world, because, once your charges are dropped, you have to beat it or get blown up yourself—as it is you can feel the explosion for yards around. Well, we dropped four—and got out of the way. As for the sub ... *zowy!* Up she came to the surface, ripped wide open. Then she stood up on her end and sank as if somebody had pulled her down by the tail.

One man of the German crew floated out of her before she sank for all time, and Ole, before we could stop him, had lashed a rope around himself and was overboard hauling him in. The German was dead, so he couldn't give us any information. Worse luck! But we didn't let that make us feel blue. I tell you we were a pretty pleased bunch. You feel good all over when you get a German sub. They are so blamed much like a crook waiting in a dark alley to stab a man in the back. You owe it to society to knock him out good and proper.

Yep, great crew ours. Some say destroyer duty takes nerve, but the reason I like it is that you don't feel like sleeping on your job; you're just too blamed afraid you'll miss the thrill of your life if you do. It's a great life! Take it from me!

Hospital Apprentice Dudley Speaks

IN TRAINING

I didn't know what I wanted to enlist in—I didn't care. All I thought about was that war was declared. That set my New England blood boiling, I suppose, and I didn't waste any time. I happened to be in Baltimore. I scooted down to a recruiting station and joined the navy.

They asked me what branch of service I wanted to go in for. I said I didn't give a hang just so long as I'd get a chance to go across and do a thing or two to the Huns. They chose the hospital corps for me. It sounded all right. I didn't dream of the hard work I was letting myself in for.

After I'd left the station I called up mother on long distance. She was visiting in Connecticut. I told her I had joined. She said she knew I would and that she was glad I had not waited a day. That's mother all over for you. I think every ancestor she ever had fought in some war or other. No slackers in this family!

It was April. I had on an unlined suit and a light cravenette when three hundred of us left Baltimore at eleven next day. We were going to Newport. At five that afternoon we took the Fall River line. It was pretty chilly then. I kept wondering why the dickens I hadn't brought along an overcoat—but you didn't speak about being cold, although I'll bet three-fourths of the men on that boat were chattering. We were in the navy now—fine sailors we'd make if we complained about a chill!

We arrived in Newport between four and five in the morning, and anchored until daybreak. I thought it would never come. The sky was grayish. I hadn't slept all night and I was beginning to wish we'd get somewhere where I could turn in for a good rest,—but no such luck.

A petty officer met us at the steamer pier, taking us over in a little government boat to Coaster Island. We landed at the Government Pier and there we lined up. There was a queer old tub anchored nearby. I asked someone what it was, and he told me that I was gazing upon the old frigate *Constellation*, which fought in the war of 1812 and is now used as a signal school. She certainly looked out of date. I wondered if our snappy sub chasers would look as clumsy as that in another hundred years.

We marched to the receiving building and stood around on the outside. I didn't know a soul there, but three of us were Hospital Corps, and we sort of stuck together. The rest were a mixture. There were "sparks" that's what they call the radio wireless men; and electricians; and there were "chips"—that's carpenters—and there were some of the "black gang," which are what the firemen are called, unless it's "coalheavers." As for us, we were the "iodine crew." It's a good name, all right.

Each draft was called in in turn. A C.P.O. would come to the door and bawl, "All right, all New York draft in," and they'd waltz in while we waited and wondered how soon before we could sleep.

After a while they called Baltimore, and we went inside, turned over our papers, and were sent to an adjoining room to receive the Navy haircut.

Say, talk about speed! Liberty motors have got nothing on those four barbers. You no sooner sat down than—*snip-snip-snip*—and—"Next!" Then you signed your name, but what the barber wanted with all our autographs I never have been able to make out. Perhaps he figures some of us may become great heroes and he'll sell the signatures for a young fortune some day.

In the adjoining room we removed our clothes so that they could be disinfected and sent home. Then we took a shower. At times the water was very warm, then suddenly it would get cold as ice. They certainly believed in variety being the spice of life.

We were vaccinated next, a long line of us. And some were so scared they just curled up and fainted. But I got through and went in for my medical exam. If you don't pass it right there you are rejected, but if you only have depressed arches, or, say, stooping shoulders, they let you through. They know navy life will fix that O. K. Just do setting up exercises for a few months and you'll gain a ton!

Then we were measured for our uniforms and they were handed out to us: two suits of winter underwear, two pair of woollen socks, a navy sweater, a blue dress uniform and two white undress uniforms, shoes, hairbrush, clothes, "*kiyi*," which, in plain English, is a clothes brush, shoe cleaning gear, needle and thread and thimble, six pocket handkerchiefs, a neckerchief, a pocket knife, two white hats, a watch cap and a flat hat. Then you get your bedding: a mattress, two pair of blankets, your hammock and your duffle-bag. Believe me, the mattress looked good to me. I could see myself drifting off into slumber in a gently swaying hammock. . . .

They marched us to a Detention Barracks. You are not supposed to leave there until you get permission, in case someone breaks out with smallpox or yellow fever.

Everything was complete in the barracks. Meals were cooked in a regular galley; there were showers, mess room and sleeping rooms. Very nifty!

A little, fat C.P.O. with a bald head came in and instructed us how to clue our hammocks. It didn't seem hard. We were pretty proud of the job—all twenty of us.

By that time we could have eaten whale oil with a relish, and a squad of four went for chow, while the other fellows pitched in and laid out the mess gear. That navy stew certainly smelled good! The squad dished us out big portions of it and that, with hot coffee, made us feel like new men.

After we had finished four men washed up the mess gear and the rest of us turned to and swept down the room. The little C.P.O. bounced in again and fixed up our watch for us—two fellows on guard, each standing two hours. The chief posted the first watchman, and taps began blowing as we started in stringing our hammocks.

It was great sport. Everyone had a theory about it, but we were told that, whatever we did, we must get the hammocks straight, because a sagging hammock is death on the back.

At nine, to the dot, lights were out. It was pitch black in our room. Somewhere outside one feeble standing light flickered, but inside, nothing doing.

Remember, these hammocks are about seven feet above ground— say, the fun started right there. How to get up in them was some problem. Each man thought of a way of doing it, and, in the first rush, one or two made it, but the rest of us only got a leg up and swung there before dropping back to earth.

Everyone was hollering suggestions and trying to get a grip on the blamed things. It wouldn't have been so hard if the hammocks hadn't moved—but they almost acted as though they had sense—hanged if they didn't. They'd bob this way and that, and the moment you got up—well——

After three or four attempts I made it. I got in all right, but, before I could settle down, over it turned with me—spilling out everything I owned, me included. I scrambled around picking up what I could in the dark, and what I said wouldn't be passed by the Board of Censors.

I piled the things in again and crawled back—pretty cautious this time. I rolled up my clothes for a pillow and lay on my back, gripping both sides of my little old bed. That's the way I slept—or rather didn't sleep. All through the night there were thump-thumps, as someone fell out and hit the deck.

When I heard reveille next morning I was so stiff I could scarcely move a muscle. I wasn't the only one though. We looked at each other and wondered if ever under the blue sky we would get the hang of sleeping in something that turned over every time you hitched a bit.

We cleaned up the quarters and spread our blankets and mattresses to air. It was bitter cold. We huddled close to the steam pipes and certainly tackled the chow for all it was worth when it appeared about six a. m.

After breakfast we lashed our hammocks, and I told mine a thing or two as I tied it up. Then we listened to the C.P.O. giving us our first talk on regulations. We wondered if we'd ever remember half the things he was telling us.

As soon as he was out of sight, in trotted the ship's tailor with a portable sewing machine. Funny little man, so intent on his tiny task of sewing little strips of white cloth inside our clothes for marking. I suppose he felt as important in his way as the navigator.

Somebody passed out stencils with our names on them, and the C.P.O., rather out of breath from scooting all over the station, dropped in long enough to tell us how to mark our clothes—then he was off on the wing. Busiest man I ever saw. I bet he lost ten pounds a morning. Well, he could afford to.

We were dying for lunch. You are always ready to eat in the navy, and the food is great. Lots of it, too. A new bunch of men had arrived—we felt like veterans as we gave them a hand at cluing their hammocks—and say, advice! We told them all there was to know about climbing into your swinging bed.

That night, when I crawled in, I found I could manage much bet-

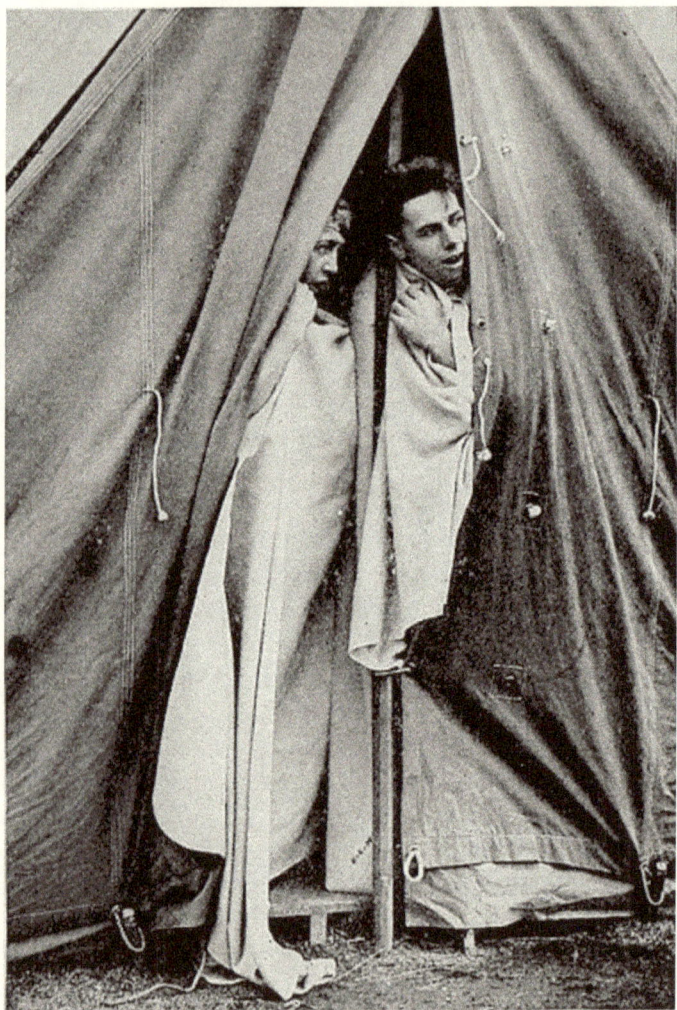

A sniff of "chow."

ter. I was dead to the world, and I slept the sleep of the just. Nothing short of reveille or an earthquake could have made me open an eye.

Next morning we parted from our room-mates. In peace times you are supposed to spend twenty-one days in detention. This was war, so we had spent three. We were to be shipped straight off to our respective division stations.

We hospital corps men reported to the head doctor and were assigned to classrooms. It seemed queer to be going to class again, after you'd been out making your living for a few years in business, but we got used to it. The lecture was on regulations, then they marched us over to Barracks B, our new home. We three from Baltimore stuck together. We were all assigned to quarters on the second deck—it's really the second floor, but you don't call them that in the navy.

It was a big place, but with a hundred and fifty men in it there was scarcely room to turn around—packed like sardines. We found a tiny space up by a window and put up our hammocks. Supper was in the mess hall, then back we'd go to school for a lecture; after that you could study or write letters until nine o'clock and taps.

We were up at five every morning, chow at six-thirty, mustered at seven-fifteen, and marched down to school in time to clean the lecture rooms inside and outside. Spick and span is the watchword of the navy. You get so you wonder how you ever lived inside of a house that didn't shine from top to bottom.

We didn't have to know much to pass exams—oh, no! Only Anatomy and Physiology, and First Aid, and Minor Surgery, and Operating Room Technique, and Nursing, and Hospital Management, and Pharmacy, and *Materia Medica*, and Toxicologies, and Chemistry, and Litter Drill, besides a little "lab" work in the compounding of medicines. Oh, no—anyone could learn that with one eye shut!

I stayed in Barracks B for three weeks, then the government sent down some big circus tents holding about one hundred and fifty, and we pitched them. We slept on cots for a change. Queer how we had to get used to them. Hanged if we didn't long for our hammocks.

I remember one night when we had a bear of a storm—a regular gale—and sure enough the old tent began to leak. I happened to be on watch so I spent about two hours going around keeping a sharp lookout for leaks—there were plenty of them. As wet a crowd of boys as I ever saw came forth, and I sent them to the lecture rooms to sleep. Funniest looking gang, sleepy and cross, their blankets around their shoulders dripping water. They made a run for the deck.

About twelve I woke my relief and started to turn in. There was no leak over my bed and I was half undressed when something rolled down my back. I beat it for the school. Not ten minutes later the whole tent collapsed, with thirty men in it. Rescue parties were formed, and the men inside needed it—a small Niagara had swept in on top of them.

But no one seemed any the worse for it. We were a hardened lot by that time. I thought of the day I had left Baltimore and the way I had shivered with the cold—here I was, only a few weeks later, only half dressed, drenched to the skin and not minding it a bit. The training had done wonders for me.

Next day a pile of lumber arrived—we carried it from the wharf to the barracks and we were informed that after school we would find nails—plenty of them—one saw and one hammer for two hundred men to lay the floor, upright and erect tents before taps. Say, that was a staggerer! But orders were orders and we fell to. What did we do? Why, we got rocks or pipes or anything you could use for a hammer and with two hundred huskies working at top speed just to show the C.O. that they can do a thing once they make up their mind to it, we got those tents up that night right as a top!

Luckily for me, my site was 'way up on Strawberry Hill, back of the hospital, and with the crackingest view of Narragansett Bay—and a distant glimpse of the Atlantic. It was a wonderful life up there. We'd become so used to outdoors that we used to talk about how strange it would feel to live in four walls again. We took everything as it came and enjoyed it. The government certainly did all in its power to make things comfortable. We used to wonder how the Sam Hill all the busy people up in Washington could keep every one of us in mind and see that we were all supplied. It is a queer feeling—that sensation that you don't have to worry about to-morrow or what it will bring, that you are clothed and fed and housed—and that your only problems are the ones that may come with the rising sun. Great life!

Other camps were all around us. The Yeoman's camp, the Seamen's camp—nothing but bluejackets from morning until night. We wondered if the whole U. S. Navy were there—it didn't seem as if there could be any more sailors in the world.

The hospital corps didn't have much drilling to do, just squad movements and litter drills and counter-marching. We used to parade through Newport to boom recruiting, and on Saturday the whole school turned out for captain's inspection on the green in front of the

War College.

There was so much to learn that we spent most of our liberties in the study hall, but once in a while we would drop in at the Army-Navy Y. M., or go down to beaches for a swim, or take in a show.

At the end of three months we were through a course that takes, as a rule, eight months. Then I went to the naval hospital and there I made my rate. Gee, but I'm glad I'm going over at last. There's a girl down in Baltimore—I've promised her some souvenirs. Some of the fellows have been back and forth eight times without a glimpse of a submarine—but I hope we see one. I'd like to tell it what I think of it.

Yes, we're leaving pretty soon now. I'll tell you all about it when I get back.

Chief Petty Officer Bertram Speaks

Zeps and Torpedoes

I joined the navy because I felt patriotic and all the rest of it. You couldn't help it down home. Everybody was doing it. My brother-in-law made the yeomanry, my chum went in for hospital corps work. Wherever you turned you found fellows discussing their branch of service and swearing it was the best in the pack. It didn't take me long to make up my mind. I sure was crazy to get "over there."

It's the English in me, I guess. Yes, I've got quite a slice. Before the war I was thirty-third in direct line for the title of Earl of Northumberland. Now I am about seventeenth.

It's queer how much I wanted to go to London. I just itched to. My family had come from Nova Scotia to Louisiana and settled there. That's where I was born—Johnny Rebs, you know. But that's ancient history—just plain all-round American now.

I never had a chance to forget the English part of me, though. I couldn't very well. You see the solicitors send me a notice every now and then telling me how good my chances are of inheriting a thirty-three-million dollar estate and a couple of dozen titles on the side.

Well, I don't care what I shipped on so long as it had a prow and a stern and kept afloat. They held me three months in the naval station waiting for a ship, and at last I got one—and what a one! An old oil tank! Ever see an oil collier? It resembles one of the countries of Europe. Which one? *Greece.*

Grease everywhere. You eat grease and you drink grease and you sleep grease and you breathe grease. You never get it off your hands or your clothes or your disposition until you land.

I was commissary. That meant I had charge of the cook and bought supplies and dished out food and made up the bill of fare. But I might as well have saved myself the trouble of that, because every little

42

thing tasted alike. Why wouldn't it, with eighty-three barrels of oil on board?

None of us wore our uniforms. What was the use? We were saving them for London or Paris, and it's lucky we did! Instead, we slapped on our overalls—"dungarees," we call them in the navy. We looked like a crowd of rough-necks, instead of a crew of snappy bluejackets.

We left some time in September, and steamed up to Nova Scotia, then across. We had a speedy ship, all right. Eight knots was the best she was known to make. Say, did it give you the jumps! It sure did! I could walk a heap faster than that old tug could steam at full speed. It seemed as though every raider and submarine in the Zone would line up in a row and take a shot or two at us—it was too easy to miss.

We had rough weather all the way. That and grease are about all that happened until we hit the Zone. There we met our convoy—a British flagship, a number of merchantmen, and a flock of torpedo-boats.

My pal was a fellow from Newark, New Jersey, Bill Willsie. He was out for excitement.

"I certainly hope something will break before we land," he'd say, "so that I can have a real yarn to spin for the folks back home."

He got his wish. It was the fourth day in the Zone, at five twenty-seven in the afternoon. I was on deck sniffing air that wasn't full of grease. Suddenly I saw the red flag go up to the mast. . . . Danger! . . . Gee, I sure did wish Bill hadn't wished for trouble out loud. I wondered which one of us would get it—the British flagship ahead of us, or the merchantmen behind.

It all happened in the fraction of a minute. I saw scudding across the water the black nose of a torpedo. You've heard of men having a premonition of death, but how about seeing it coming straight toward you at the rate of thirty miles an hour!

My God! I'll never forget it! I thought my heart had stopped beating. I gripped the railing and waited. She struck the flagship and sank her in seven and a half minutes. To this day I can see her going down—the explosion—the roar—the sudden list—the boats lowered, and, on the bridge, two figures pacing—pacing—the captain and the admiral.

Do you think they left their ship? Not they! Up and down—up and down—those two paced. Oh, I tell you the British are a great people, but I wished to God, as I stood there, that I had never had to see it proved to me that way.

43

Up and down they walked, talking together as though nothing out of the way were happening. I saw the ship settle for her last heave. No, they didn't leave her bridge. Why not? They were true British naval officers, that's the answer. They sank with her.

By that time every alarm on our ship was sounded—five long whistles, electric bells, a regular bedlam let loose. I never heard such a noise. The life-boats swung out ready to drop. All hands were on deck except the engineers. They stand by in the engine room until a ship is struck. As soon as she is hit their job is to put out the fires and turn off the water—that is, if they aren't blown into the middle of next week first.

About eighty yards away the submarine came up and fired point blank at us. She missed us again and she submerged. That was the last we saw of her. The destroyers were working like little flashes of lightning, picking up the men in the water, darting here and there. You've seen those dragon flies in the pools—that's what the little gray fellows were, dragon flies—here, there, everywhere. I never saw such quick work.

Along about eight we pulled into Dover. All dark, except for a few smothered lights. We anchored and went up on deck. We were pretty glad to have land so near. You felt a lot safer. The comfort didn't last long, for we heard the queerest buzz in the sky above us—a long hum.

"Zeps! By Cracky!" yelled Bill in my ear. "We're in for an air raid!"

Out of the blackness of the city before us leaped a million lights, cutting the darkness like a knife, hunting—hunting for those Zeps. Searchlights turning their yellow blaze on the sky, whisking from one point to another, relentless in their scour of the heavens.

Now and then they would spot one of the great black bugs that buzzed on high with that tormenting hum keep it for a second in the radius of light, losing it as suddenly, and all the while the machine guns in the city pop-popped without taking a breath.

Now and then from the sky would be hurled a black something that flamed and thundered as it struck earth. . . . Bombs!. . . Their red glare lighting up a roof—a cornice—a water front—showing groups of frenzied little black figures scurrying to shelter—then blackness once more and the pop-popping of the machine guns, spiteful, biting sound that never paused.

It lasted about half an hour. The Zeps circled Dover and went back.

The Colt gun is an important weapon for landing parties.

The guns stopped firing one by one, as though they had run down. The lights died out, save for a few on guard. Did we sleep well? We did not, in spite of the fact that we hadn't had our clothes off a single night while in the Zone.

"I bet we're going to have a swell time in London," Bill told me. "We sure have started off right!" We certainly had!

We had three days shore leave and we started out next day—sixteen of us—in our best bibs and tuckers, to see the sights. Were we glad to get ashore? Chorus—we were! We took a little train—funniest train I ever saw. Reminded me of the Jim Crow cars back home. They were divided into first, second and third class, but over there uniforms can ride wherever they choose, and we are expected to pay only half of a third-class fare.

Remember, we were one of the first shipload of American sailors to put foot in London, and as such we were one of the sights of the city. Crowds! Say! New Year's Eve around Times Square or Mardi Gras back home had nothing on the mob we drew there in Charing Cross.

They fought to see us. They elbowed and pushed and wormed their way in. The girls threw their arms around us and kissed us, and the men cheered, but that wasn't all. They wanted to wish on the eagles on our sleeve—all of them did. And they wanted souvenirs—anything for souvenirs—buttons or American loose change.

"Give us American dimes," they'd cry. "Give us American dimes," and they fought for them. I had some Confederate money with me. They snapped it up.

Two bobbies—they are the English policemen, you know—came to our rescue, and packed us into taxies, but not before the crowd surged around us exclaiming about our caps—our little white canvas hats. They had never seen any like them. They wanted those, too. I don't know what would have become of us if the police hadn't taken a hand.

Say, by that time, we were hungry and thirsty, but we didn't dare get out for fear of starting another young mob. I felt like the President on inauguration day, or the king, or someone.

"Stop at a beanery," yelled Bill to our driver, a little old man with round shoulders and a shiny coat. He cocked an eye at us.

"Beg pardon, sir?" he said.

Bill replied, "As me Allies, the French, put it, '*Jay fame.*'"

Our driver wasn't a French scholar. He looked at me.

"Where is it you want to go, sir?"

"Food," I said. "In plain Anglo-Saxon, I hunger—I crave nourishment."

"Oh," he said, "I see, sir," and he dumped us out before a restaurant. We went in.

"Ham and eggs," we all shouted. Every good American sailor always orders that, but our waiter didn't care.

"You can have either ham, sir, or eggs. Not both."

And we learned something else, too. You couldn't order more than thirty cents' worth of food at one sitting. It's against the law, and, what's more, you can't treat a pal; you can't even treat a girl, which ought to please some people I know back home.

We didn't stay in that joint. We tried four others with the same result. I never wanted to spend money so badly before in my life.

What got me was the work the women are doing in London. Women bus drivers—women street cleaners—women baggage smashers—and all of them the healthiest lot of girls I've ever seen— red cheeks and clear eyes and a smile for us always.

"Will you let us wish on you?" they'd cry. Of course we let them. I only hope their wishes came true.

But, say, night in London is one great party. It gets dusk, and, if you're on to what you are in for, you make a bee-line for where you are going, before the light fades entirely—or you don't get there. We didn't know that, so we planned to go to the Hippodrome; but we waited until dark. Say, talk about pitch black! It's pale beside London at night!

Imagine Broadway with not a single light—not even a pale glimmer. Imagine it filled with thousands and thousands of people, bumping into each other—talking, laughing, whispering.

No wagons or street-cars—nothing on wheels, except an ambulance, which crawls about with weird blue lights, very dim. Just crowds and crowds, knocking your hat off, stepping on your feet, taking your arm by mistake. Men apologizing. Girls giggling. Voices coming from nowhere. Forms brushing by and vanishing.

The streets are full. I think every last person in London must turn out after dark. It is one big adventure. You never forget it. You don't know where you are or where you are going—no one seems to. When you get tired you stop someone and ask the way to a rooming house. If they know they lead you along. You feel a door. You open it and close it cautiously behind yourself. You are in a dark vestibule. You cross a black hall groping before you. Suddenly your hand touches two curtains drawn close. You part them. Beyond is light at last. You enter the living-room of the house. Someone quietly draws the curtains so no faintest glimmer will penetrate the outer darkness. Say, it was some experience!

Next day a gentleman in a big motor picked us up, five of us, and showed us the sights. He wouldn't tell us who he was, but he was a big bug all right. All the bobbies came to a crack salute as he passed by, and he took us through Parliament and to Buckingham Palace. We couldn't find out his name. All he confessed to was that he sat in the House of Lords; so I asked him about the family estate. He knew all the facts but said none of the crowd were in London just then. I thought of looking them up, but I didn't get a chance.

That night we took in the Hippodrome. It was all right, but it made us homesick for the one on Forty-fourth Street. When we got back to the ship next day we found we were going home to the U.S.A. That was the best news I ever heard.

We came back in sixteen days. Say, do I want to go over again? Well, rather! And I'll take a longer shore leave next time. Perhaps I'll run up to Northumberland and look over the old place. After all, seventeenth isn't so far down the line, now is it?

Captain Barclay of the Marine Corps Speaks

"The Leather Necks"

I don't want to say anything that sounds like boasting, but the Marine Corps is the finest branch of service in the world. No exceptions. I guess you know that marines date back to days of ancient Greece. They had them then. They were the landing party on shipboard—the fighting force. They were right there with their bows and arrows and javelins and spears, and they carried out their contract as well as the men who rowed the ship. Each one had his own particular duties. It's the same today, but somehow the nation has got into the habit of saying, "*Leave it to the Marines*"—and we've tried to prove that we are worthy of the trust.

In the old days there used to be a bit of feeling between the sailor and the marine. You'll find the reason for it in English history. About 1803 there was a mutiny in the British navy, and the marines helped put it down. After that they were called the Royal Marines, but the sailors got an idea that they were on board a ship to prevent mutiny and they did not like them any too well. But they soon found that the marine had his own field—and that he had just one motto—"*There's nothing I can't do.*"

It's funny the way our men tackle everything, particularly as they have never been specialized like other branches. For instance, there is no bridge-building company, yet over and over again when there has been need of bridges the marines have just gone out and made them.

There's nothing you can think of that you won't find some of them can do, from getting up a dance to rounding up a bandit. I was in Santo Domingo with my company. Most of the men were recruits, pretty soft from life in the barracks. We were ordered to a nearby post

49

on the trail of a desperado. Before us lay a march of about four or five days. A hike is all right over level country that is fairly dry, but ours lay through a series of marshes winding upward over a mountain.

We started off at a brisk pace and we didn't let up. There were patches of land which sent us through mud up to our knees—our feet were never dry day or night—but there was no kick coming about that. We were going to reach our base at the time planned—no later.

The last day was the worst. We were on a level stretch at last, but there was no shade, and the sun beat down like a ball of fire. Our wet shoes dried and cracked on our feet—and we were blistered from heel to toe. But that didn't prevent our making thirty miles that day or doing the last four miles in forty-five minutes.

We were tired to death when we reached our destination. It was ten o'clock at night. The men dropped where they halted, just about all in. We hadn't been there fifteen minutes when word came to us of the bandit we were rounding up. It seems he was in hiding in the hills about twenty miles north of us. A woman brought us the tip. He had thrown her down and she was taking her revenge in the usual way.

There was no mistaking her earnestness. There was just one thing to do—go out after that rebel. I sent over to the men and asked for seven volunteers. When the boys heard what was wanted, sixty per cent of the whole company offered to go. They forgot they were tired, stiff, sore—you couldn't hold them back!

I had the horses saddled and everyone who could commandeer an animal mounted one. Some of them had never been on a horse's back before, but that did not stop them. They were off like a shot, the whole crowd of them—thundering up that dark road in search of the outlaw.

They caught him, too, after an all-night ride, and they brought him back with them. I tell you a good rest was coming to them after that. They certainly needed it!

The men have a great pride in our service. They show it outwardly by keeping themselves trim as a whistle. On shipboard each man is allowed a bucket of water a day for his ablutions—no more. Well, a marine makes that bucket go a long way; with it he washes himself, brushes his teeth, cleans his clothes, and scrubs the deck—anyone who claims he can do more than that with a bucket of water will have to show me!

And a marine takes his job seriously, whatever it is—yes, indeed. In the little French towns in which they have been landed they have become the traffic cops of the place. All the duties of a *gendarme* have been assumed by them with neatness and despatch.

The marines decided that no bluejacket was to hold conversation with a French girl. Once that was definitely passed upon they began enforcing the law. A particularly happy young bluejacket had received a flower from the hands of a little French maiden. She had pinned it to his coat. Along came the marine while Jack Tar was trying to thank her in his very best and limited French.

"Cut it out!" growled the marine.

"You beat it!" said the bluejacket.

In reply the marine quietly but quickly plucked off the flower to emphasize his command. There was nothing else to do but to fight, and the marine managed to beat up Jack mildly. Jack went to the ship's doctor to have a stitch or two taken in his ear. He was still raging, and vowed he'd get that marine as soon as he was out. The doctor stopped stitching long enough to look up over his glasses.

"I wouldn't, if I were you," he said, "that marine was very gentle with you. Next time he might do some real damage."

Yes, the sailor respects the marine as a majesty of the law. One slim, young marine is enough to make a gay and irresponsible party of bluejackets along the docks sit up and take notice.

There was a young sergeant by the name of Watson. He was a particularly efficient chap. Seats were hard to get on the train going up to Paris, and, when a party of army, navy and marine officers arrived at the little station, we found that Watson had reserved seats for all of us. On our return trip we were surprised to meet him at a station some distance from the little town that he was policing. We asked him if he, too, had been up to Paris.

"Yes, sir," he said. We asked him how it happened he was so far away from his post.

"I went up on my own, sir," he told us calmly enough. "I got to thinking that, perhaps, the bluejackets were starting something in Paris, and I thought I'd take a run up just to see they weren't putting anything over on the marine corps."

Evidently he found everything O. K. or he would have remained to adjust it.

It was Watson who had such trouble making the French peasants clean up their huts. Now, as everyone knows, the French peasant is an individual who wishes to be left alone to tend his little patch of ground. It is his own business if he has the cow beneath the same roof

51

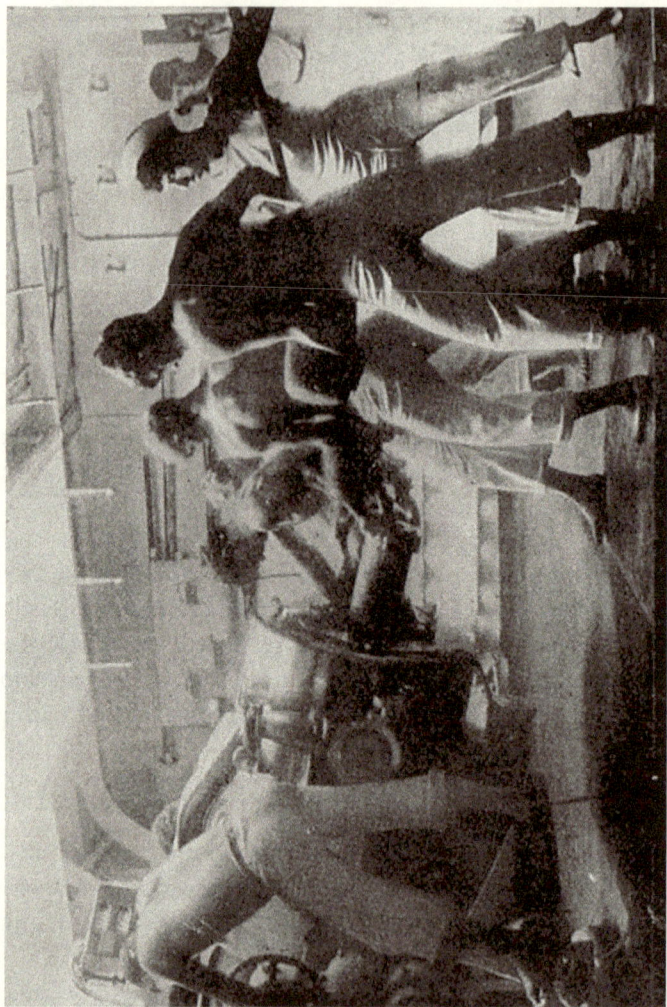

"STAND BY!" —GETTING READY FOR FRITZ.

that covers him, and if the chickens have the freedom of the house it is, after all, an affair between himself and his poultry, so to speak. But not in Watson's eyes. He had orders to clean up that town, and there were no exceptions. Protests were in vain. He saw that sanitary conditions for the first time prevailed, and not until the houses fairly shone, and the streets resembled Spotless Town, did he relax and express himself.

"I see their point of view, of course, sir," he told me, "but if it happens to be the wrong point of view there's nothing to do but to right it."

The marines aren't beaten often at any sport, but when they are they take it as a tragedy. A ship's crew had been trained to shoot. They knew they could shoot, and, on landing, they challenged the marines to a contest. The marines, under a grizzled old sergeant, long in the service, were immensely proud of their skill on the range. They accepted the challenge. They were dead sure of the outcome. There wasn't a nickel within hailing distance that wasn't wagered!

The marines got on the range before the bluejackets. No advantage was taken. Well, the bluejackets beat them at slow fire. They beat them at rapid fire. They beat them on skirmish, which the marines had boasted most about. Altogether, it was an unhappy day for the marines.

Next day the commander of the ship, rising very early, saw a sight which fascinated him beyond words. On the range were the crack shots of the Marine Corps. Glowering above them stood the sergeant, his beard fairly bristling with anger, his back ram-rod straight. He had the men all out, and he was teaching them, with a thoroughness incomparable, the rudiments of rifle practice.

With stony faces the men submitted to the insult of being returned to the kindergarten of shooting. Again and again they went through the manual. It was a just punishment for permitting bluejackets to defeat them!

"*Join the Marines—and see the world*"—and to do that our boys pride themselves on extra quick obedience to orders, for there is no telling when an expedition will be pulled up in a hurry and sent to the other end of the globe. But whether they go or whether they stay, they accept it all calmly.

The words of the little marine, who was plying his shovel one hot day, seem to sum up their contentment. He had been shovelling dirt since early morning. The sun was warm, and he paused in his task to mop his face. He looked up with a grin.

"I enlisted to see the earth," he said; "and here I am, digging it up, turning it over, and looking at it!. . ."

Bugler Colby Speaks

The Way With the Frenchies

I'm a home-loving man. I don't ask anything better of life than my little house in the country, with the wife bustling about and the kids waiting for a game of ball or a tramp in the woods.

Yes, I'm a peace-lover, but I'm the kind of peace-lover who wouldn't quit this war a minute before the German empire is wiped off the map. I'm going to stand by until that day comes to pass—as come it will!

I'd like to tear the heart out of every German for the work they have done to the French and British and Scotch and Irish—oh, I know what I'm talking about. Yes, you do, if you stay in Havre long enough. You can get all your facts first hand.

Just wander down to the station every other evening when the big seven-thirty express thunders in with her load of returned British prisoners. Yes, you can see with your own two eyes what German methods are, and I tell you it makes a man, who is a man, ready to give the last drop of blood in him to stamp out a nation that treats men that way—and what's worse—women and children. . . .

I'd been in the navy five years as a bugler. You are on the bridge all the time, standing by for duty. We were assigned to one of the prettiest yachts afloat. It was originally the famous pleasure boat of a great New York multi-millionaire. She certainly was a nifty craft—about three hundred feet long, almost as big as a destroyer, and graceful as a swan in the water.

There must have been great parties aboard her in the old days, and I wonder how she felt when they knocked out her mahogany state-rooms and hauled down her real lace curtains and tore up her fine saloons, for transport duty.

Nothing classy about her then—just dirt and grease and the smell

55

of pork and beans. As for her colour, she was gray, same as any little ten-cent tug. But her lines didn't change. She was like a fine lady who takes off her ball gown and puts on rags, and in spite of it you can tell she's a fine lady through and through.

We carried the first American troops to land in France. The very first. That was making history, wasn't it? It seemed right and fit that the proud little yacht should have the glory of taking the first batch of Yankees to foreign shores.

It was a rough trip, though, and we felt sorry for the boys whose sea travels had been limited to the ferryboat between Hoboken and New York. Rough weather on shipboard is no joke. You can talk about the hardships of the trenches, but how about being aboard a pitching vessel, when you can't even get a light in your galley ranges, which means no food can be cooked and a steady diet of hard tack and bully beef?

Oh, we hadn't any kick coming. It was all part of the game, but we did wish the sea would calm down a bit and the fog lift. I never saw such a fog in all my days. From the minute we left, it wrapped itself around us like a damp blanket. You could hardly see your hand before your face. We didn't need a smoke curtain that trip—nature provided one for us, all made to order.

Our first taste of excitement was on the thirteenth day out. We were just wishing for something, when we saw, through the mist that had let up a little, a strange ship ahead of us. We signalled her to make her colours, but instead she started off as though she were trying to run away. That promised hot excitement, so we went after her. We chased her for five hours—now losing her in the fog, now sighting her again, gaining on her inch by inch. We were sure she was a blamed German merchant vessel trying to sneak back to her base, and we had the guns primed to send her straight to the place all Germans come from.

When we got within a few hundred yards of her we hauled up the battle ensign on the foremast. We meant business. The gunners stood by. Just as they expected to hear the command, "Fire when ready," up came the British Jack to her mast!

Say, but we felt foolish, chasing one of our own allies all over the broad Atlantic. We asked her why the deuce she hadn't made her colours before, and she signalled back that she was under the impression we were an enemy raider.

We calmed down after that and made port without pursuing the rest of the British navy to cover.

The base we established was the first naval base in France. We kind of like to think that some day, when our grandchildren cross the Atlantic on a pleasure trip—it having been made safe by us from those German vipers—they'll hunt out the little harbour, tucked away in a corner, where their grandfathers landed that June day, and went ashore with the first handful of American soldiers to set foot in France. They were there for just one purpose—to show what red, white and blue blood could do toward making the world a safe place to live in.

No fogs in France—just yellow sunshine and soft air and eager crowds waiting for us with open arms. Flags everywhere. It certainly made you catch your breath to see your own star-spangled banner flying from the windows of the little French town.

We went ashore pretty flush. Some of us had as much as a couple of hundred dollars, I suppose. We made our way to the railroad station. We wanted to get up to the "gay Paree" we'd been hearing about all our lives. We couldn't believe we were within hailing distance of it. It had always been a bright red spot on the map that we hoped to visit some day—and here we were just a few hours away from the liveliest city of Europe.

We made for the railroad station double quick. It was there I had my first real taste of French big-heartedness. In the crowd I noticed a beautifully dressed woman. She had all the French zip about her, but when she saw us she began to cry, and she just let the tears roll down her cheeks as though she didn't know she was doing it.

She stepped forward as we were passing, and the crowd let her through. They seemed to know who she was, for they whispered together and pointed her out. She hurried toward us and began to talk in broken English.

"You must be careful," she begged us. "All this money you have—it may tempt some of these poor people. Put it away, I implore you. Use only as much as you need. . . ."

Then she caught my hands. "Oh, how glad I am that you have come at last! How I bless you and your country!"

She bought our tickets to Paris for us and saw us safely on the train, putting us wise to the ropes. Nothing was too much trouble for her to do for us. I tell you we never forgot it. Even after the train pulled out of the station we could see her standing a little apart from the rest, waving her lace handkerchief to us until we rounded a curve and lost her from sight.

Now that we were started on our journey we felt great and I began to tune up. I can sing a little, my mates say, so I let out a few songs that made us think of home. While I was giving them "'Way Down upon the Suwanee River" the door of the compartment opened and a big chap in a British uniform stood there grinning.

"Don't stop, boys," he said. "It sounds bully!"

It was Paul Rainey, the great hunter. Say, we certainly were glad to meet him, not only because he spoke our language, but because we knew from hearsay that he wasn't afraid of man or beast, and that's the kind of a fellow you like to know. He stayed with us the rest of the journey, and as he was to be in Paris a day on his way to Belgium, he took us with him to the American Ambulance Quarters, where he was stationed.

We arrived there in the evening. Next day he had to go on, so we found ourselves wandering around the Place de la Concorde and the Place Vendôme and the Champs Elysées without compass or rudder.

It was a pretty city, but all of a sudden I felt awfully blue. Everywhere you turned somebody hollered something at you in a language you couldn't make head or tail of—even the hack drivers and little kids in the street talked French.

I took a room at the Continental, and say, they almost robbed the shirt off me. Next morning I was wishing so hard for home you could almost hear me coming down the street. I found the American Express office and lingered there listening to people speaking English. I wondered where the gay part of "Paree" came in. It looked busy and prosperous and warlike to me—but gay? Nothing doing.

Just then someone spoke in my mother tongue and I whirled to see a French army officer at my elbow.

"If you have not already seen the sights of Paris, it will give me great pleasure to show them to you," he said.

I hadn't, so he proceeded to do the honours, and, like everything the French do—be it big or small—he made a thorough job of it. He was my host for two days and a half, and I'll guarantee I saw every little thing in Paris from the Apaches up. I wouldn't have missed that sight-seeing trip for all the gold in Europe. That's the French for you. Their hearts and their homes were opened wide to us. I bet there isn't a Yank living who wouldn't fight to the last breath for them.

Next I fell in with two French privates on furlough. They took me home with them and to show my gratitude I sang our songs for them and taught them some real live United States slang. They were good

58

"Before taking" — a dose of military discipline makes them "Topnotch Americans."

pupils, too, and were proud as peacocks of startling a crowd by calling out, "Wash you step!"

It was from them that I bought my best little souvenir—a German officer's helmet one of the Frenchies had picked up after shooting his man. It was a peach of a helmet, slashed across the patent leather crown, and still stained with blood. Inside was stamped the officer's name and regiment. He was of the Death Head Huzzars—the *Kaiser's* own.

I asked Frenchie if he didn't want to keep it, but he shrugged. He could get plenty more, I made out he meant. He was going back to the front soon; they'd be picking helmets off the trees once the French got really started. So I bought it from him for forty *francs*.

Our boat lay in the harbour. They were coaling it, and, once ready, we started our work of patrolling the coast. It was on one early afternoon that we got sudden orders to put to sea, and we started out at a fast clip. Somebody passed the word that we were on a rescue party and to keep a sharp watch out for rafts or lifeboats.

Rescue party! Ever see men who have faced death in a leaky boat all through a black night? I'll never forget their faces—something was stamped there that will never come out—a grim, strained, white look you don't like to see. The few boats we spotted bobbed about like corks on the waves. The men were too numb to pull on their oars. They had been rowing all night. Some of them were half dressed.

Once we pulled them in and helped fit them out with clothes we heard their story. They had been struck amidships by a blasted torpedo along about midnight. Their boat was a yacht something like our own; the impact of the shell blew her to a thousand bits. The men asleep were killed like rats in a trap. The few on deck managed to launch some boats and rafts before they were sucked down with the vessel.

That midnight attack made our score against the Hun a little higher, not that I needed any incentive to hate him another notch. I had a vision stamped on my mind I could never forget. I could still see that black snake of a train crawling into the crowded station at Havre— hear the long-drawn grinding of the brakes and hissing of steam—see the guards keeping back the mob surging forward for a chance to welcome home its sons. There was endless noise and confusion—but occasionally you would find a silent watcher—a woman and sometimes a man, who stood motionless, staring at the cars—muscles taut, waiting for God knows what horror.

Yes, you don't forget the first sight of the returned prisoners, in their worn uniforms. White-faced boys looking about eagerly for the face of friends—friends at last, after three long years! No, you never forget those battle-scarred men, with here an arm gone, or a leg—or worse, the eyes blinded forever.

Oh, my God! you dream of it nights afterward; you see that endless line of maimed and broken men. . . .

Hate Germans! I tell you I'm a peace-loving man and all I want is my little home, with the wife and the kids, but do you think I'd stop fighting in this war while there is yet a drop of blood left in me? Not much! I love my own too well to let them suffer as those French and Belgian women have—that's the answer!

Ensign Stafford Speaks

A Yankee Stands By

I haven't anything to tell about. Being torpedoed is an old story now. Any number of men have met Fritz on the way over, and, if they haven't been quick enough, he's managed to take a shot at them, but it isn't often we fail to get a chance to return fire. Just let a periscope stick its head out of water, and I'll show you action on deck that would make a Kansas cyclone look tame—not that I've seen one. My home is in the East. The best we can boast about is a blizzard or two, and a sixty-mile gale.

I enlisted as a signalman, and was assigned to duty on a merchant ship. There were two other U. S. N. signalmen aboard her, and we managed to make the time fly talking about home and the people we knew.

One of our prize ways of speeding up a long evening on shipboard was to swap notes on the summers we had spent. We all three, at different times, had "vacated" in the Maine woods, almost at the identical spot, and, do you know, we hailed the fact with something very close to triumph!

I guess we three hashed over every little incident of our trips. We found we had had the same close-mouthed Indian guide, that we had all fished on the same bank of a little lost lake, that we had all camped on the same site in a clearing by the water. But when we discovered that we had used the same sort of tackle, and the same-sized rifles, we were almost "moved to tears," as the lady novelists put it.

Those things, small as they seem, are the most important things in the world when you are far away from home. They certainly make men inseparable, and, aside from the fact that Dick Chamberlain and Tod Carlin and I were the only Americans aboard, we became, from the first, the best pals in the world.

We were proceeding as flagship of a convoy, and, as such, we kept an extra sharp lookout for trouble, once we were in the zone.

It was three o'clock on the afternoon of a clear September day. The sea was smooth and we were all on deck. The sky was so blue and the sun so bright that it seemed as though the lurking submarine we were always expecting was a myth like the sea serpent you read about but never see. Night time is the time you are looking for an attack, but broad daylight always seems to dispel thoughts of danger. However, the danger was there.

We were struck close by the engine rooms. All I remember clearly was the terrific roar and splintering of wood, and the sudden listing of the ship. The order rang out to clear the ship and the crew immediately took to the life-boats in the event of rapid settling.

We three found ourselves assigned to the same life-boat. There was a slight delay in lowering it. That delay was fatal. The explosion that we had been expecting blew our boat to pieces and we found ourselves struggling in the water.

The officers' boat had been lowered and it drew up alongside of us. They helped us in. The captain was all for going back to his ship. He was sure there was no immediate danger of her sinking. The watertight compartments fore and aft were holding and he called for volunteers to go aboard and help in an attempt to beach the ship.

By this time the other life-boats were beyond hailing distance and we found out afterward that the men in them, including some British gunners, were picked up later by patrol boats.

Of course, all the occupants of the remaining boats volunteered. I didn't particularly like the looks of the ship, as her well docks were on the sea level, but she had stopped settling and we followed the rest aboard.

It seemed queer to be on her again. There were just a handful of us, the rest of our mates were out of sight, bound for none of us knew where. It was like returning to a ghost ship, she lay so still on the waters, rocking softly, the waves washing over her deck.

There was plenty of work for all hands—it didn't give us time to think. I was glad of that. Dick and Tod and I joked a bit about what the people back home would say now, if they could see us up to our ankles in water on a sinking ship. Afternoon changed to evening. Still we saw no sign of help coming toward us. However, just so long as Fritz stayed away we were satisfied. When it got good and dark, though, we weren't quite so pleased. It helps, I can tell you, to be able to see your hand before your face. You feel a lot happier then.

Late that night we made out something coming toward us. We weren't sure whether it was friend or foe. It gave us a bad few minutes, then we made out the towboats who had come to our assistance. We were so glad to see them that we almost cheered out loud, which is one thing you don't do in the Zone.

We passed them lines, and they steered a course for land. All this time our ship was slowly working water; you could tell it by measuring, but the chief engineer continued to assure the captain that we would be successful in beaching her.

All night we moved slowly through the water, wondering each minute when she would take a sudden dive to the bottom. Walking along the edge of a canyon in the dark is much the same sensation, I guess. We were glad when we saw a pale streak in the sky, and watched the morning star fade. Daybreak found us still afloat.

Some of the British crew had had experience on torpedoed ships. I suppose they knew that the wise thing to do was to leave her if they got the chance. That was the reason why they chose to go on the escort vessel when the captain put it up to them. By morning it certainly looked as if our ship would never be beached on this earth. We were in water up to our knees. There wasn't a dry spot on us, and the chill winds that swept down from the north played a game of hide-and-seek through our wet clothes.

The captain called us all together. He told us that the chances for bringing her in were small, that no man need stand by, that he did not blame anyone for choosing dry land and dry clothes in preference to almost certain sinking.

His speech did not shake the officers' determination to remain aboard her—all of them. They simply had no intention of getting off so long as there was a glimmer of a chance of landing her safe. Then the captain asked Dick if he desired to remain or if he wanted to get off. Dick grinned.

"I'll stay, sir," he said.

The captain asked Tod.

"I'll stay, too, sir," he answered.

The captain came to me. I had my answer ready.

"I'll stay, sir," I told him.

After he had thanked us and gone on, Dick called a meeting of the Three Yanks. "You didn't stand by just because I volunteered to, did you?" he asked anxiously. We shook our heads. Our teeth were chattering so that it was hard to say what we thought, so we didn't try. What I thought was something to the effect that I wished I had my extra sweater on underneath, and that I was glad I had two such plucky pals.

We spent another night on board her. We had had not slept for forty-eight hours, but we didn't seem to need to—the excitement of wondering what the next minute would bring banished sleep.

The following morning at four o'clock we landed safely on the beach. The destroyers took us off the ship—all we knew was that at last we were on something where we could rest. I remember some of the crew asking us questions, but I don't remember our answering. We just dropped down on a roll of blankets and closed our eyes. . . .

I woke last. Dick and Tod were chatting softly in a corner. I opened my eyes and listened.

"Well, write it down, Tod, so you don't forget," Dick was saying. "You and Clink and I will hike it for Maine. Is that straight?"

"What's this?" I asked. Dick grinned over at me.

"We're making a little date for after the war," he said. "We figured what a lot we'd have to talk about on that camping trip, eh?"

I nodded. "You can count me in," I said.

But, as it's turned out, there won't be any camping trip for the three of us after all. Dick was lost at sea on his next trip across, while I was sick in hospital. Then I heard that Tod had gone down, and it nearly knocked me out. There never were two such pals as those chaps.

Perhaps some day when it's all over, and we've licked the Hun to a standstill, I'll wander up there myself with our stony-faced guide; and perhaps I'll sit on the bank of our little lake and fish in the clear water with the tackle we all used, or shoot the same-sized rifle—and I'll have the satisfaction of knowing that they've trod every inch of the ground—it will be almost like having them there—but not quite— pals like that don't happen more than once in a lifetime—I wish I could tell you just what great sort of fellows they were—oh, well, I couldn't if I tried a thousand years—so what's the use?

HERE'S TO THE MARINES—THE FOREMOST MILITARY BODY IN AMERICA!

Seaman Burke Speaks

A Taste of Hell

I joined the navy as an apprentice seaman. I thought it would be great to try a new way of licking the Huns. I had sampled the army. Yes, I was at the Somme with the Canucks. Greatest bunch of fighters the world has ever seen!

I can say it, because I'm an American, but as soon as war was declared, my three cousins and I beat it for Canada and enlisted. We were all in the same regiment, the third to go across.

You've no idea until you get into the thick of a fight with shrapnel whistling past you and shells bursting a few feet away, how much depends on your leader. It's up to him to win or lose the ground you're holding for all you're worth. The men in charge of us were young and some of them pretty green at the war game—but say! there wasn't a bloody Hun alive that could scare them! Not by a long sight!

We sailed in August, about two thousand of us. We had a quiet trip across and, oh, Christmas! how we did long to get into the scrap! They landed us at a French port and we had just three days' training before we were ordered up.

You can't make much headway in three days to prepare you to meet the Boches, but we did manage to get in a little drilling and skirmishing. All the bayonet charging I learned was from a Jap in my company. He was a funny little cuss. Why he joined up I can't imagine. You'd think he would rather save his skin and stay at home, but he was all for fighting. He had been trained in Japan and had joined the Canadians at the last minute.

My cousins and I learned all we knew from him. He seemed glad to show us. He was a friendly little chap and some fighter! I remember seeing him alongside of me for a few seconds in a trench full of Germans . . . and then not seeing him. What became of him I never knew.

You don't, most of the time.

A long line of troop trains were awaiting us. Pullmans? I guess not!—freights. We piled in. We were all anxious to get to the front. We knew they were in desperate need of men and that we might get a chance to go over the top, green as we were.

It was night before they opened the doors and let us out. We seemed to be in a sort of meadow. It was black as a cave, except for the lights of the station. There was plenty of noise as two thousand men alighted, but there was another sound—a dull, thick booming . . . cannons! It seemed thousands of miles away, but you never forgot it for an instant. It meant that we fellows who had been so recently in offices plugging away for so much a week were out there at last on the great battlefield of France!

We had reached the trenches. They weren't at all like I supposed they'd be. I expected them to be narrow, with room enough for one man only. Instead two and sometimes three could walk abreast. It seemed to me as though we marched a hundred miles that night. I was so tired I was ready to drop, and then all the mud I had ever read about seemed to be planted in that trench! Mud! We tramped through knee-deep slime—knee-deep, mind you—and we thought that was bad until we went in up to our waists.

It must have been raining pitchforks before we arrived, and as we scuffed along the best way we could it began again—a cold, driving rain straight down from the black sky, stinging our faces and running down our necks. After a while we halted for the night.

There were dugouts where you could set up your cook-stove if you were lucky enough to own one. All your food you carried on your back in cans, but you didn't have energy enough left to open them. You just dropped down under the shelter of a bunch of sand-bags if you were lucky, or if you weren't, in a muddy patch of ground where you slept like a log.

Next day we were on our way—that long line of drenched men tramping toward the sound of the big guns. That's how you measured distance, by increasing volume. The rain had begun in earnest and it never let up for the three days we made our way to the trench just back of the Big Hill.

It seemed to be our destination, because we got orders to begin digging, and we went to work with pick and shovel. I forgot how tired I was in the excitement of being so near the Huns. You do out there. You don't worry about dying, that's one sure bet, nor about eating or sleeping; the one thing that gets you is when your best pals go west.

I had to stand watch that night. That meant two hours of pacing back and forth, fifteen feet, ready for the enemy's charge at any second. I couldn't believe that the fellows we were waiting for were so close up—there across that short patch of ground—but I realized it when a shell fell not five feet away from me and blew three of my pals to bits. By God! I knew it then!

I shall never forget it. I'd been listening to them talk in a little knot as I paced by, swapping smokes and trying to find a dry place to stand. One of them laughed. That was the last sound I heard before the crash of exploding shell. There wasn't one of them left.

We were four days waiting for the signal to charge. We were mad for it. It seemed as if the leaders could not hold us back another day. We wanted to get at those damned Huns who had killed our pals. We knew we could lick them, raw as we were. We had some full-blooded Indians from Ontario with us. They were the real thing in a fight. They did not know what fear meant. There just wasn't any such word in the language for them, and when they charged they forgot they were supposed to use rifles. They threw them away and drew their long knives—razor-sharp. That's how they went after the Huns—and butchered the swine good and proper.

On the fourth day the signal was passed along the trench for a charge. One hundred and fifty men were picked—every third man. I was lucky and was one of the number. Every man was keen to be first over the top. About nine of the Indians came along. None of my cousins made it, but the little Jap who had taught me bayoneting was beside me, grinning and fondling his rifle as a mother does her baby.

Our leaders sprang up on the sand bags and hurled us the order. How few of them came back from that charge on which they set out so fearlessly!

We climbed up. We heard our officers shouting to us and our comrades wishing us the best of luck, to give the Huns hell! We sprang forward and the Germans opened a rain of bullets from their machine guns full upon us and the men who followed. They swept our lines. Men reeled and fell to the left and right of me—just crumpled up like those little toys whose springs have snapped. Still we went on. We made the trench and I speared my first Boche. Got him, too! Brought back his iron cross as a trophy. The Germans were scampering to the next trench like rats caught in a trap. They sure do hate hand-to-hand fighting!

We held that trench six days. It was jumpy work. The Germans were driven back, but there was no telling when they would start with the hand-grenades. They didn't do that, but they did something worse—gas. It was pretty new to us then. We were fitted out with a sort of rubber mask that wasn't much good. We saw a fellow drop a way down the line. Then one of the brownish trench rats, a friendly little chap, who ate the scraps I shelled out to him, turned up his toes. We clapped on our masks, but the wind was with Fritz and the gas swept through our trench on the breeze.

It lasted about an hour and a half. I'd hate the job of being the first man ordered to take off his mask and test the air for the rest, but someone has to, and it often means lights out for him.

I had been slightly wounded—a sabre cut on my leg, but I managed to dress it myself. It was ten times better to be up, however rocky you felt, than lying around those damp trenches. I wondered where my cousins were. I worried about them. Somehow I wasn't afraid for myself, but I just wished it would soon be over and I could get home. You think about home an awful lot out there.

We were sent to some swamps next. There were cement trenches—German make—and they were considerably drier. We were pretty comfortable there except for an occasional shell blowing things to bits. I used to wonder how there was enough lead in the world to make all the shells the armies used. We always had plenty of ammunition. The Russians were the ones who got the raw deal. We passed a lot of them on our way out front. A regiment of them was holding a square. They were dull-eyed boys—hopeless looking. Do you blame them? One day they would be sent out with ammunition to burn. The next they wouldn't even be given a rifle. How did they protect themselves? Oh, rocks and stones, I suppose. But they were wiped out when they tried to charge empty-handed, that's sure.

The Germans raided us with hand grenades one night. We heard them coming and we fought like fiends, but they outnumbered us five to one. I went down with a shot in my side. The next thing I remembered was being aboard a transport bound for home. Nothing ever sounded so good to me as that word! I found my three cousins were aboard. One of them had lost his two legs, another his leg and his arm, and the youngest had his right arm blown off.

It didn't take me long to find out how lucky I was. All I needed to do was to look around at the other eighteen hundred wounded. They landed us at Halifax, on our way to Toronto. I was laid up for quite a while, and the funny thing was now that I was home again I kept planning ways to get back as soon as I could just to show those Huns who's who.

I used to lie in my clean white bed, looking out a long window onto the garden. It was calm and quiet. But I didn't seem to see it— what I saw were those blood-soaked trenches, with your pals gasping out their lives alongside of you and your leaders, falling even as they urged you to charge! It took me a while to get well and when I did I went back to the States. I had an idea. I would join the navy. It would be a new way of meeting Fritz. I liked the thought of killing him wholesale on the sea.

I enlisted as an apprenticed seaman,—that was last March. I am in fine trim, except for a scar on my leg and a bullet hole in my side. I've finished training now and I'm ready to be shipped across. Gee, but I hope we'll get a fat submarine full of German officers—and that we'll drown them like the rats they are!

Second-Class Gunner's Mate Fowler Speaks

The Wanderlust and the War

I've been torpedoed three times—three ships gone down under me, and I'm still here. Didn't mind it much—I can swim; besides, I'm pretty used to the sea—first shipped when I was thirteen. My father and mother had sent me to a manual training school. I didn't like it. I was always playing hooky and finally ran away.

I didn't care where I went just so long as it was on a ship. I knew it was the sea I wanted. Before I decided, I used to hang around the docks. I liked the smell of the water and the big talk of the old salts who had been around the world a dozen times. They didn't stay cooped up in any four walls studying geography—they went out and lived it.

I knew enough about sailing to ship as boatswain. I was big for my age, so they took me on. It was a sand sucker going down to the mouth of the Mississippi.

The skipper took a kind of a shine to me. He saw I wanted to study navigation so he lent me books and let me go into the chart house and work. Arithmetic was hard for me, and spelling, too, but I'd copy out words I didn't know and take them to him. I guess he saw I was in earnest.

As a result I got my rate as able-bodied seaman when I was fifteen. I was in New Orleans then, and I saw a chance to ship on one of the Standard Oil boats bound for Tampico.

I was crazy to go to Mexico. There was a "Mex" on the old ship and he was always talking about the sunshine and free fruit in his country. When I told him where I was bound for he wanted to come, too, but my new skipper couldn't see him. "Mex" drank too much fire

A MARINE CAN DO ANYTHING—EVEN RIDE A HORSE!

water for the good of one man.

We didn't stay long in Mexico. I got a chance to go through Vera Cruz, and that was about all, before starting for home. I'd saved quite a lot of money and all the way back to New York I kept asking myself would I or wouldn't I drop in on my father and mother to let them know I was alive. I couldn't decide. When I got to New York the first thing I did was to buy myself a great outfit; then I started to the street where I knew the family lived. On the way I met a pal who was shipping on a small boat leaving for Canada. He wanted me to go along. There didn't seem to be any good reason to refuse, seeing as I had all my papers. I'd never been to Canada.

I told him about wanting to call on my parents, but he said there'd be time enough when I got back to port. I went along with him and up to Nova Scotia.

All the time I told myself it was going to be my last trip up the coast. I wanted to see Europe next. When we came back to New York I went up to Union Hall and told them I'd like to ship across. I got my wish. They sent me on a Standard Oil steamer bound for Rouen. At last I was going to France!

I liked that country from the start. The first sight I had of it was white houses and green fields and church steeples. I was so busy looking at the scenery I couldn't do a stroke of work. I got liberty to go up to Paris, and I saw all of it for two francs. I just hopped into one of those little cabs and said to the driver "Giddap," and he rode me around. I didn't miss a thing.

We went back to Norfolk, where we were quarantined for seven days because a yellow cook we had broke out with the same color fever. That gave me time to think, and I made up my mind that I'd pay off and go up and see my folks. I was sixteen then, hard as nails and pretty prosperous.

Once ashore I bought myself everything from patent leather shoes to a derby hat. I wanted them to see I'd made good.

I walked in on them at dinner time. My father didn't know me, but my mother did. "It's George!" she hollered, then stared at me. But father didn't. He wanted to lick me for staying away all those years. Mother wouldn't let him, though. She wanted to hear all about where I'd been. I was glad I could put some money in the bank for her. I stayed home about two weeks and then got so restless I knew I'd better leave before they threw me out.

Well, I let myself in for an adventure that time for I went to Halifax, and from there shipped on an oil collier bound for Mexico. We struck a hurricane and were washed ashore. That was my first shipwreck. We had to eat stores out of the ship's supplies, which were pretty low at the time. I didn't like the looks of things and I decided to foot it into Tampico, which we figured wasn't more than forty-two miles south of us.

Eight of my mates and I figured that by travelling toward the sun, we'd make it in a couple of days. We packed our grub and put on the good heavy Dutch sea boots we wore in heavy weather, and set out through the woods.

Hot! Say, your head blistered under your cap. We struck a swamp, but we were afraid to go back—it was just as bad as going forward—so we started through, but we miscalculated, for we spent a whole day and night in there before we got our bearings.

We climbed the branches of the trees at nights and slept as best we could in them. But two of the fellows caught the jungle fever, and one of them died before we could get him out. We buried him there and marked the place.

Another man was pretty sick, and I remember reading somewhere that sassafras root was good for fever. We found some growing there, and we managed to build a fire—but we didn't have matches to light it, so we struck flints until we got a blaze. We cooked the root and gave him the juice. It saved him.

On the outskirts of the swamp we saw a little Mexican house. It was the greatest sight I ever want to see. The woman was cooking some kind of meat over her fire. We didn't stop to inquire what it was so long as it was *f-o-o-d*. That was enough for us. She was glad to give us all she had, because American money goes big down there. Several of the men stayed to look after our sick mate, but I hot-footed it into Tampico to find the consul and try to get back to the States. I found him but he couldn't do anything for us.

I didn't care much. It was a pleasant country, so I decided to stay. I was there six months. At last I grew tired of everlasting hot weather so I asked a skipper on an English ship if he'd take me back to the States. I told him I didn't care about the pay, just so long as I got home. That impressed him and he signed me up for a quarter a month. He couldn't have paid me less, but what difference did it make to me? Wasn't I getting out of that all-fired hot country?

We docked at Baltimore. I was pretty seedy, so I took the first job I could get, which was night watchman on the docks. Then I wired my mother that I was stranded without clothes or money. She sent it double quick. I knew she would.

Once I was outfitted I applied for a third mate's job. I had already made my license, although I was only seventeen. The hard thing was getting any skipper to believe I knew all I claimed I did. I found one at last. I told him to fire any questions at me he could think of. He sure did. He asked me things a chief has to know and I came through. He took me on as third and I paid off at New York.

When I reached there I went to the seamen's Bethal, where I got clothes and the chance to ship on an English vessel bound for the other side. That was in 1915. The German subs had started their little game of hide-and-seek, but we didn't expect any trouble. However Fritz was waiting for us. It was about six o'clock in the evening, dark, with a full moon. I was on deck watching the moonlight on the water. It's a sight I never get tired of. All was quiet except the throbbing of our own engines, when suddenly we felt the blow that ripped her side open. A torpedo had registered a hit.

We couldn't see the sub; she had gotten in the moon's rays, and it was impossible to make her out. We didn't try. The order, "abandon ship," had sounded, but I didn't make a lifeboat; instead I dived off the side of the ship and swam around in the water for a few minutes before somebody heard me yelling and yanked me in.

Next morning an English schooner picked us up and we went ashore. Say, but I was mad through to think of a blinking submarine sinking a neutral. I never was neutral from that minute, and when we got into the war I went in the navy. I knew that would be the one place I'd have a chance to take a shot at the Kaiser's pets.

We carried a big cargo over; our cargo line was 'way down. We had a lot of green hands aboard, "hay-shakers," I call them. Some of the boys were pretty seasick. I bet they wished they had never started across.

Well, we delivered our cargo and started back, when sure enough, one dark night, we got it again. This time, though, I was standing under the bridge, and in the explosion a piece of rail was hurled against me that broke both legs.

A big Swede, who had always a hand out to help everybody, hoisted me into a lifeboat, but in launching it was smashed up. I was in the water and I certainly thought my last hour had come, but I found the big Swede was swimming beside me, and he dragged me onto a piece of board floating by. I lay there until it was light and in answer to our

S. O. S., American destroyers came on and picked up our boats. Was I glad to see the good old American flag? *Was* I! I didn't know much when they hauled me aboard—the pain was pretty bad, but they sent me to a hospital over there, and before long I was around again, fine as ever. Takes more than a German sub to keep me down.

I went back to the States in style on a transport. As I always carried my Union book I had no trouble in getting another new outfit, once I reached my home port. I set out for France on a cargo vessel. Well, say, it was clear sailing over. We met our convoy and they hoisted up their signal flag. We were all of two hours making it out. At last we could read it, it spelled:

"What are you doing,—bringing Brooklyn Bridge over with you?" They were making fun of our queer-shaped bridge. Well, we started back, but I know things always happened in threes so I was pretty sure we'd get it going home. I was right.

It was my watch, late in the afternoon. I was keeping a sharp lookout when I saw the torpedo scudding toward us.

"Wake of a torpedo in starboard bow!" I yelled. Say, that vessel wheeled like a streak—and the torpedo missed. But the next one didn't. Bing!—I felt the big ship quiver under me, and the explosion that followed blew me so high that I came down in the paint locker with my arm under me.

You'd think I'd be used to torpedoing by this time, and could keep my sea legs under fire, but I didn't. I'm getting better though, and I'm waiting to get a shot at Fritz that will send him where he'll stay for a while. I certainly am glad every time I hear we've sunk one of them, but I always wish I was one of the crew of that lucky ship.

Chief Nurse Stevens Speaks

UNDER THE RED CROSS BANNER

I was educated abroad. That's how I came to love France and England almost as well as my own country. I was in my teens when I returned to America. I had always wanted to be a nurse. Even while at school I longed for the days when I should be old enough to begin training. It was my calling, and, when I left school, I answered it.

I trained in France, England and America. I had practised but a short while when I married. My husband was a surgeon, and from him I learned more of nursing than I could ever hoped to have acquired from text-books. We were always together. We played and worked and travelled all over the world. When he died, it was like a great light going out. I did not know where to turn—I did not know what to do. Even to this day I cannot get used to his being away from me. It always seems as though he were on one of his professional trips and would return.

And then in 1914, just six months after his death, war came, and I knew that my place was in France, so I sailed at once and enlisted in the nursing corps.

Those were the days before the great base hospitals were established—the days when the dead and wounded were left in piles awaiting such care as could be given them by the handful of overworked doctors and nurses.

It was there I found my "son." We had come to a group of white-faced boys—the mark of death on their brow. Lying a little apart from the others was a young Frenchman. He had an ugly shrapnel wound on his shoulder. He was unconscious when we found him, but he was so appealing, so young, that my heart went out to him. His clothes were stained with dirt and blood, and the mud was caked on his cheek, where he had fallen.

Torpedoes cost money—they are often recovered and fired again.

When we moved in, he opened his eyes. "*Maman*," he said, and smiled at me. I think that was what won me completely.

I watched over his convalescence and learned that his own mother was not living, so when he was well once more and ready to return to duty, I adopted him as my "*fils de guerre*," and to this day I hear from him twice a month—and such letters! Full of his battles and his play at the rest billets—his dreams and his hopes. He is France at her best, with the love of youth and life and country in his heart.

There were sights on that battlefield you never forget—never. It was the bodies of Frenchwomen left dead by the Germans that haunt me—the women they dragged from captured France and took with them to their trenches. We used to thank God when we came upon these girls that we found them dead. At least these few were out of their unfathomable depths of misery at last.

After ten months of nursing in France, the doctors ordered a rest—no—commanded it, so I left the service and went to England to visit an old schoolmate, now married. Her husband was at the front, but her father, a peer, whose name is a great one in England, lived with her.

He had known me since childhood. He was very fond of me. He was a man of great importance to the government, but he had a delightful way of dropping all the cares of State, once he reached home, and of romping with his two tiny grandsons whom he adored.

In their home I found the quiet I craved, and, as I grew stronger, I longed to get back once more to duty. I knew so well the desperate need for trained workers. My friends sensed my growing restlessness and Violet's father spoke of it at dinner one evening.

"Why not join the British Army?" he asked me. "I'll try to get you a good post."

There were a number of guests present, and, as Sir Arthur sat quite far from me, I did not catch what he had said. But Violet had. She leaned across and called to me.

"You aren't listening to father—he means you." I turned toward him eagerly. "Why not join the British ranks?" he repeated. "You say you feel fit again and want to get out there. Well, I'll give you a chance to prove it."

I didn't believe he half meant it, for his eyes twinkled; but I caught at it.

"I cannot get to the front soon enough to please me," I cried. "Just try me and see," and no more was said about it.

The days passed and the lovely English summer changed into autumn. I felt splendidly. One day I came in from a long walk. I glowed with health. I just knew that I could not remain idle another instant. I found Violet in the nursery with her babies. I told her I must go. She laughed at me.

"So long as you feel that way, it's fortunate this letter came for you this morning, isn't it?" and she laid in my hands a long, official-looking document, bearing the royal coat-of-arms in one corner. I tore it open. It was a command to appear before the Matron-in-Chief of Her Majesty's army. I knew by the time that I had finished reading it that Sir Arthur was responsible in a large measure. He was well aware of the fact that no neutral could serve in the Allied armies unless by royal order. I flew to the office of the matron-in-chief. My knees knocked together. Could I qualify in her eyes for a post at the front?

What transpired seemed like a golden dream to me. I was appointed chief nurse—or matron, as they call us Over There—of a hospital ship holding four thousand beds! I did not show my inward tremors. If it could be done, I was going to do it—I, an American—and what was more I was going to make those British nurses on my staff love me in spite of themselves. I dared not think how afraid I was to tackle it. I just kept saying, "I'll do it! I've *got* to, so I can."

I returned to Violet and dropped in a heap on a couch.

"What's happened?" she demanded—and I told her. She listened, her eyes like stars.

"How splendid! You can do it if anyone in the world can! You've proved your worth in France. Oh, I am so happy that you are to look after our poor boys!"

Sir Arthur came in at this moment. I knew by his smile that he had been listening.

"Well, well, so you are to be a matron, are you?" he teased. I nodded. I was past speech.

"Perhaps you don't know that you will be gazetted as major in the British Army as well. That will probably be your official rank."

And a major I became on my floating hospital. I felt strangely alone at first. The only American among so many English. For the first time in my life I longed for my compatriots. Then one day as we lay at anchor in the harbour, I saw, some distance away, a battleship flying from her mast the Stars and Stripes. I began to cry, I was so glad to see my own flag again. I asked our wireless operator if he would send her a message.

"Will you ask an American officer aboard the man-o'-war to come aboard the British hospital ship and speak with an American woman?" The instrument snapped the message. The battleship caught it, and, a few hours later, I saw an American naval officer for the first time in over a year.

I had never met him before, but I was so glad to talk with him of our own land that I dreaded the time when he must return to his ship. He went at length, and I followed him with my binoculars. It gave me a warm feeling around my heart to have a Yankee ship so close by.

Once I started to work in earnest, I found that my nurses were eager to co-operate with me in every way. Instead of resenting my authority over them, they were anxious to help me, and the fear I felt of my ability to handle this great task was swallowed up by the mountains of work before me. There was no time to fear or to rejoice. There was no time for self, with four thousand souls aboard who needed caring for each hour of the day and night. For our ship was loaded with the wounded from that desperate fighting in the Dardanelles.

There were a great *per cent* who came to us with hands and feet cruelly frozen, from the weeks and even months in icy trenches. Then there were shell-shock cases. One which appealed to us all was of a chaplain, adored by his regiment. Through the heaviest fire he had stood by his flock with no thought for his own safety. An exploding shell had brought on that strange state of aphasia. He did what he was told to do docilely and quietly, but he remembered nothing that had gone before.

He was sent back to London, his mind still clouded. I used to think of him often—his quiet, studious face and soldierly bearing and his eyes with their eternal question in them, which none of us could answer for him.

Months later I saw him again. The government was in need of a matron to take charge of a four-hundred-and-fifty-bed ship bound for South Africa. Fierce battles were raging in Mesopotamia. I was selected for the task. I had eight nurses and a hospital corps of fifty.

As I came aboard her, I saw a familiar figure standing by the gangplank. I caught my breath. It was the chaplain himself. There he stood, smiling quietly, with hands outstretched.

"I am going with you, matron," he told me, "to care for the boys."

He was well once more and back again in the field.

Malaria was rampant in Africa. Our ship exceeded capacity by over a hundred cases—men with raging fevers. Working at top speed, we could not bathe them all, and cold baths alone could save them.

The convalescent officers helped us. We worked like machines. Some of the nurses caught the tropical fever, too, but they stuck by their post. They did not dare give in. There were too many sick and dying men calling for them. I have known those girls to stand on their feet when their own temperatures ranged between 103 and 104 degrees. They laughed at the idea of giving in. They couldn't. That was all.

You have heard of the brutality of the Turk. Let me tell you he is gentle compared to the ferocity of the Germans. We lay at anchor near Salonika. The Turks were on one side of the Gulf, the British on the other. More than once I have seen the Turks hoist a white flag to us, and, when we have at length replied to it with our flag of truce, they have sent an envoy aboard. Always, he desired to parley with the matron instead of with the commander, and I would be summoned to receive his message.

"*Mem Sahib*," he would say, "we are about to open fire on the British. You will move your ship about fifty yards. You will then be out of danger." He would bow and return to his regiment, giving us ample time to move before the great guns roared once more.

But the Germans! To bomb a field hospital or shell an ambulance, or sink a Red Cross ship is a triumph for them!

It was three o'clock one morning. We lay in the Mediterranean. An accident case needed instant care. I ran to prepare the "theatre," as we call the operating room. The patient was treated and had been lifted to a stretcher when the Huns' torpedo struck us.

Then came the crash, the sudden trembling of the ship and the sudden dreadful listing. We carried the man to the deck, scrambling up as best we could. The engine had not been struck, but the stern was shattered. Every man who was able to, reached the deck with life-belt on, and the nurses and doctors flew to the rescue of those below.

We carried them all on deck, and the commander faced us quietly.

"The boats on the port side are smashed, and those on starboard cannot be lowered."

There was not a sound for a full moment after he spoke, as the awful truth dawned upon us. Then his voice rang out:

"There is only one chance—to jump for your lives."

Jump for your lives! I looked at the men who were too ill to be moved, who lay unconscious, with flushed cheeks and closed eyes.

Jump for our lives! What chance had they? Truly the Boches could take toll that night if they counted sick and wounded men and Red Cross nurses as fair prey. . . .

The commander shouted to us: "Jump feet first. Watch out—jump *feet first.*"

We had practised doing it in the tank on the way over. With life-belts on, it is the only way of preserving your balance.

The men were dragging out tables and tearing up planks for rafts. They hurled them into the water, and little groups of them climbed the rail, stood poised an instant above the black depths below them—then leaped down. . . .

The voices of hundreds of struggling men rang in on our ears and we were helpless to aid them.

The commander called the nurses to him.

"You go next," he told them. "The matron and I will jump last."

They were the bravest, coolest lot of girls I have ever seen. They climbed the rail, hand in hand. They hesitated a second—with a shudder at what lay before them, then they leaped forward. . . . I could not look. Only the commander and I remained. He drew me to the rail.

"I can't do it," I cried, drawing back. But he was very firm.

"Come," he said quietly, "it will soon be too late."

He helped me up. My heart was thumping like a trip-hammer in my breast. I could not—I could not—*could not* jump. He drew me down suddenly. I lost my footing and plunged after him. The water closed over me. It seemed hours before I came to the top. For a long time I could not move. At length I began to swim. I knew enough to get as far away as I could from the suction that would draw me as the ship sank.

Three hours later patrols picked us up.

And yet, I love the water. If I am ashore and cannot sleep, I pretend my room is a cabin and that I am on a quietly rocking sea. That is why I entered the navy nurse corps of my country when she declared war on Germany.

So I have served under three flags since war was declared, and at last—at last I am under my own!

Gunner's Mate M'quire Speaks

"ABANDON SHIP!"

Me father was always talkin' about the old country. Sure and he said there was nothin' in the whole of America to compare with a corner of County Cork! We kids used to poke fun at him, but I'm confessin' it made us kinder hanker to see that land ourselves.

He was after claimin' that the grass was greener there than anywhere else on earth and the sky bluer. As a kid I planned to run away and ship over there just to see if the old man was givin' it to us straight. But it was to Canada I drifted, and, because I have more inches than most men, the Northwest Mounted sent me an engraved invitation askin' me to join them, which I did for six years.

Sure, it's a great way to spend your days, ridin' through snow and ice or mud and mosquitoes—accordin' to the season—after the gang of outlaws runnin' loose up there. But it was always worryin', the wife was, for fear I couldn't shoot quick enough and they'd get the drop on me. She'd tell me that it was the kid she was considerin'—she wasn't wantin' to bring him up without a father. She'd say he was too big a handful for her to manage, then get around me by claimin' he was a chip off the old block all right—all right.

So I give up me post in the Northwest and settled down in Winnipeg. Then the war came and I could see reasons all over the place for me joinin' up at once. First of all, though me country was America, me home was in Canada and I knew that nine-tenths of the Canucks would be friends of mine. Then secondly, wasn't I Irish, which meant gettin' into any scrap that was goin', so help me?

Well, the wife held me back at the start. She kept coaxin' me to bide a bit. She argued the States wasn't in trouble yet, so I listened with one ear, but with the other I was hearin' from all sides about the greatest free-for-all fight in the world's history, and I knew that me,

85

"Gas Masked," the men in the trenches throw hand grenades.

Patrick M'Quire, had no business to be standin' by.

The wife wasn't well and she was always frettin' at the thought of me enlistin', so I told her I'd wait, but I warned her that it was entirely responsible she'd be if Germany tied the Allies in a show-down. I told her I was a sharpshooter with a record in the Northwest to be proud of. I asked her why she was keepin' me back. Sure, I demanded what business she had to be hamperin' the Allies' chances like that!

Well, me humour fell on deaf ears and I stayed until me own country, the United States of America, declared war, and that same afternoon, by the grace of God, I walked meself up, bought tickets for the States, packed me family aboard and two days later joined the navy.

It's compromisin' I was when I joined. I told the wife that the fear of trenches or gas attacks need never enter her heart, but I knew as well as me own name the danger on the seas of Fritz gettin' playful and stickin' a torpedo in your ribs—but why worry her?

Better than me prayers I knew firearms. I could take a rifle apart and put it together again with me eyes closed. I had had as many machine guns jam on me as the next fellow. I was entirely qualified to be a gunner's mate, which, I assure you, I wasted no time becomin'.

They shipped me over on a British auxiliary—a cargo ship. For the two months they held me at the trainin' station. The wife had been knittin' and knittin'! If I'd been bound straight for the North Pole I couldn't be after havin' more helmets or sweaters or socks or wristlets than she sent me. Whist! how these women do slave for us. It was askin' her not to, that I did first, until I saw it was givin' her the only mite of pleasure she could squeeze out of me goin' away. Women is like that. They wants to be babyin' their men folks until the end of the story.

What I valued most of all was a picture she had taken with the kid. That nearly finished me. I was after winkin' and blinkin' over it like an old fool parted from his senses. But she looked so sweet smilin' at me there and the kid looked so clean it almost broke me up.

I set sail on a warm June day. There was no chance to go home and say goodbye. In a way I was glad of that. She was, too. It's rough weather we had all the way and plenty of work, but I liked the life. I was hard as nails. I was strong from bein' outdoors twenty-nine years of me thirty. Weather didn't worry me—rain or shine was all the same.

We came to the Zone. "Aha!" says I to meself, "so this is the patch Fritz has picked to try his luck with us as a target!" I kept wishin' for a sight of him. Sure, I stayed awake nights worryin' for fear the convoy sent out to meet us would be so good it would scare all the subs away. It was nearin' the point where we expected the sub chasers to meet us that I got me wish.

It was about five in the afternoon with the sun goin' down like a red balloon, when we sighted a raft with a barrel propped up at one end. There were two fellows aboard her, in a bad way from the looks of them, stripped to their waists, wavin' their shirts to us for help.

We had been after hearin' how dangerous it was to stop your engine in the Zone and rescue survivors, but good God! who'd have the heart to pass those poor fellows by! Perhaps they had wives and kids at home same as us. We drew up about five hundred yards from them and started to lower the boat when the raft rose out of the water and turned over and the men dived off. Under it we saw the deck of a submarine, the barrel still on her periscope.

It's trapped we were by her dirty trick! She struck us amidships and then submerged. There wasn't time to fire. We were sinkin' stern first. The boats were swung down and I started to get into me own when I remembered the wife's picture! Sure, I had to have it! There wasn't no two ways about it. I just wouldn't get off the ship without it. Someone called to me to come on. Someone pulled me arm. But I tore it loose.

"It's goin' back I am," I told him.

"You're crazy! She'll be down in four minutes."

"I tell you, it's goin' back I am. . . ."

And he let me go. I guess he thought he'd done his best to save a poor loon. All hands were on deck. I made for the hatchway and found it fillin' with water. The furniture was floatin' around like the little toys the kid puts in the bath tub.

I fought me way to me bunk. Over it I'd nailed the picture. I felt with me hands until I found it. I tore it off the wall and stuffed it in me shirt, then I started out. The water was clean up to me waist and pourin' in. The force of it sent the chairs and tables crashin' against the wall. I dodged them and found the stairs. They were submerged. It's on me hands and knees I crawled, until I reached the top. The water poured in on me.

I found the deck deserted. I looked down. A few boats were bobbin' on the waves. I dived off. When I came up it did me eyes good to see a boat a few yards away. I swam toward it and they pulled me in. A seaman named Doyle and another called Hooper were good strokes. They rowed all eighteen of us away out when the cruiser went down.

About a hundred yards from us was a boat full of our officers. It was decidin' to follow them we were, when the submarine came to surface again. She was after knowin' which boat held officers, too—no doubt about that, because she trained her machine gun on the lot of them without wastin' time, and opened fire. Yes, by God! shootin' on men adrift in a lifeboat!

That's a sample of Hun fightin' I won't forget in a hurry! I'd have given me life and that of all me dear ones just then for a chance to cut the throats of those cool devils on her deck, pumpin' death into that boat load of helpless youngsters. . . .

We expected to get it next and it's ready for them we were. I hoped with all me heart and soul that they'd come close enough to hear the names I was callin' them. But they didn't honour us—not them. They figured that we were all enlisted men, not worth wastin' a shot on, for they submerged.

It was growin' dark, but there was still light enough for us to take stock of our fodder. All lifeboats are well equipped—provided with ten gallon barrels of water, and with tins of bacon and crackers. It's glad to find the food and water we were. The chances were pretty fair of our bein' rescued in a day or two. That was good, seein' we hadn't a compass and most of us was green. We couldn't even pick the stars and none of us knew seamanship.

We could do nothin' but wait until mornin' and pray for the sight of a sail. Mornin' came. We were stiff, 'part from wet clothes and 'part from the hard boards on which we'd been lyin'.

There were four boys aboard—just kids, not more than eighteen or nineteen. It's game they were, all right. They were the life of that gang. It's "Cheer up, they'll find us today," they'd tell us.

One of them was bubblin' over with spirits. He was a big, blond kid called Terry. He was one of the gun's crew and I'd liked him from the start. He appointed himself C. P. O. in charge of the chow and dished out the crackers and bacon to us, jokin' about our *table de hôte* and sayin' he'd try to do better next meal.

Some of the older men aboard shook their heads over the way we was eatin'.

"Better hold back on the rations and water," they warned us. "We ain't rescued yet."

But we laughed them down. We felt sure some ship must have caught our S. O. S. the night before. It stood to reason help was hurryin' toward us.

We took turns scannin' the horizon. It wasn't hard, because the sky was cloudy. We didn't say so, but it's hopin' we were that there wouldn't be a squall. It wasn't long before the water grew choppy and a mist came up. Some of the men were glooms for fair.

"Fog risin'. We couldn't see a ship if she was alongside of us," they growled.

The boys wouldn't be downed.

"We'll shout just to show them we're here," they said, and, at intervals all that long night, their voices rang out, but no answer did we get.

Along toward mornin' it began to rain in earnest. We caught the raindrops in our mouths. We decided to start economizin' in water. It cleared up the third day and the sun came out. It burned our wet faces. Some of the men slept, but most of us kept a lookout. Help must be comin' soon. We didn't know in what direction land lay. Sure, we'd pull toward the north, then hold a council and decide it was the wrong way after all, so we'd start off due east. But we didn't row as hard as we had the first day—not by a long sight. Some of the men were against goin' away too far from the place where our ship went down.

"If we'd stayed around there we'd have been picked up by now."

The men were gettin' sulky, blamin' each other.

"Sure, if you'd listened to me——" we all started off.

Only Terry didn't get sore. He and the other three kids wouldn't give up hopin'.

"Oh, they'll find us by another day," he'd grin. "What's bitin' you all?"

The fourth day dawned and slipped by. No help. The fifth day came, and with it a storm that tossed our boat from the crest of one big wave to another. The water washed over us in torrents. We bailed like madmen to keep afloat at all.

Sure, now, it's queer when you come to think of it, how hard men will work just to keep that little spark of life inside of them. With no hope in view they won't give up while there is strength in them to go on with the fight.

We proved it through those days of black horror, in an open boat on a sea full of salt water. That was the awful fact that stared us in the face as the days slid by—no gettin' away from it—a certain knowledge that the water in those barrels was gettin' lower and lower.

Six days—seven days—eight days. . . . Over a week adrift, drenched to your skin all the time, cold as ice at nights and hot as fire by day. Crackers and bacon . . . bacon and crackers . . . and not enough of either to last much longer—and then what? . . .

We didn't talk much. Even the kids, when they weren't asleep in a sort of stupor, would stare out at sea. Then on one mornin' we made out smoke on the horizon! It was an hour of rejoicin'. We were that wild with joy we stood up and yelled until our voices cracked. We raised our wet shirts on an oar and waved them, but it was no use. The smoke vanished, they had never seen us.

Some of the men sat down and cried like babies. I wanted to, God knows, but it's responsible I felt for those youngsters. Now supposin', I'd keep tellin' meself, that one of them was me own kid. Would I be after lettin' him see that I'd be givin' up all hope? Not much I wouldn't, so I tried to cheer them along.

Half a cup of water a day was each man's portion. Half a cup, when you're burnin' up with thirst and there's water all around you. Just what you're longin' for and it's cool and wet and—salty. We knew it would lead to madness to drink that stuff, but we all wondered in our hearts how long before we would have to.

We found if we sucked on buttons it helped a little to keep our dry throats moist, but our tongues were swollen and our lips were parched.

There was a Norwegian aboard. He had been torpedoed before. He had great ideas as to what we ought to do, but the trouble was he couldn't speak English, and none of us knew Norwegian, so we couldn't get him at all.

Nine days—ten days—eleven days . . . the water in the barrels was down so low that I tried reducin' me drink to a quarter of a cup a day. It was then I got on to the fact that Terry was actin' queer. The Norwegian put me wise. He pointed to the ocean and patted his mouth, then he jerked his thumb at Terry. I called the boy up sharp.

"Drinkin' salt water, eh?" I snapped.

He looked up. "What's that to you?" His eyes looked hot and feverish, his cheeks were flushed.

"You cut it out," I ordered. I almost choked as I said it. What if it had been me own kid?

"All right," he growled.

But he didn't stop. At night he scooped up cupfuls of it—he and the other youngsters, and one mornin' we had four ravin', crazy boys on our hands. They were stronger than we were and when they tried to jump overboard we couldn't stop them. We did our best to save them, but they fought us with the strength of fiends. We couldn't get them back into the boat—we lost all four of them. After that I don't remember much.

For two weeks the water held out, but we were afloat four days longer. We were semi-conscious by that time—nothin' troubled us.

An English fishin' smack picked us up and took us to a lighthouse off the Irish coast. When I came to I found meself bein' fed water a spoonful at a time. Sure, I couldn't take more if I wanted to, me tongue was that thick. I stayed there three weeks, when they sent me to Ireland and I lay in hospital there for a month. From the windows I could see the treetops and a glimpse of the heavens, but do you know it seemed to me that the sky in America was a heap bluer and the leaves a world greener and, oh, how I wished for a sight of the wife and the kid!

So they brought me home and here I am. I'm not after sayin' me father was a prevaricator—no, indeed! But I *am* sayin' that where your folks is there will your heart be also, and, take it from me, the fellow who wrote, "There's no place like home" knew what he was talkin' about! There ain't—be it County Cork or old New York!

Chief Pharmacist's Mate Hall Speaks

PRISONERS OF WAR

I want to be a doctor, that's why when the war came I turned to the Hospital Corps. I had heard of the advantages you derive from the instruction and the experience you get in that branch of service, and, besides, I liked the crowd of men going in for it. One high school had its whole football team in the corps. I figured if it was good enough for a star quarter-back it was good enough for yours truly.

I went in as an apprentice, of course, but I soon got onto the fact that I needn't stay one for the rest of my life if I really wanted to get ahead. Naturally it meant work and lots of it, but why stay in the "pick-and-shovel" class if you don't have to?

You see, advancement entailed certain responsibility. To be a pharmacist's mate third class, you are supposed to be of immediate value to the medical officer in the sick bay of a ship. Once you are a pharmacist's mate second class, you are supposed to take charge of a hospital corps man's work on board ship, and in case the medical officer is away for the time being. But to be a pharmacist mate first class, it may be up to you to take charge of the medical department of a ship to which no medical officer is attached.

I went to it. I don't suppose I ever worked so hard in my entire life. But I didn't see the use of being in a corps and staying down in the coal hole when there was plenty of room on top.

Our duties could be summed up briefly: we nursed the sick, and administered first aid to accident cases. Some of us were to accompany expeditionary forces to the front and give first aid to the wounded, beside assisting at surgical operations. That was about all we had to do, except to look after the medical stores and property, and know all there was to know about compounding medicine.

But one of the things I liked best about it was a certain fact that

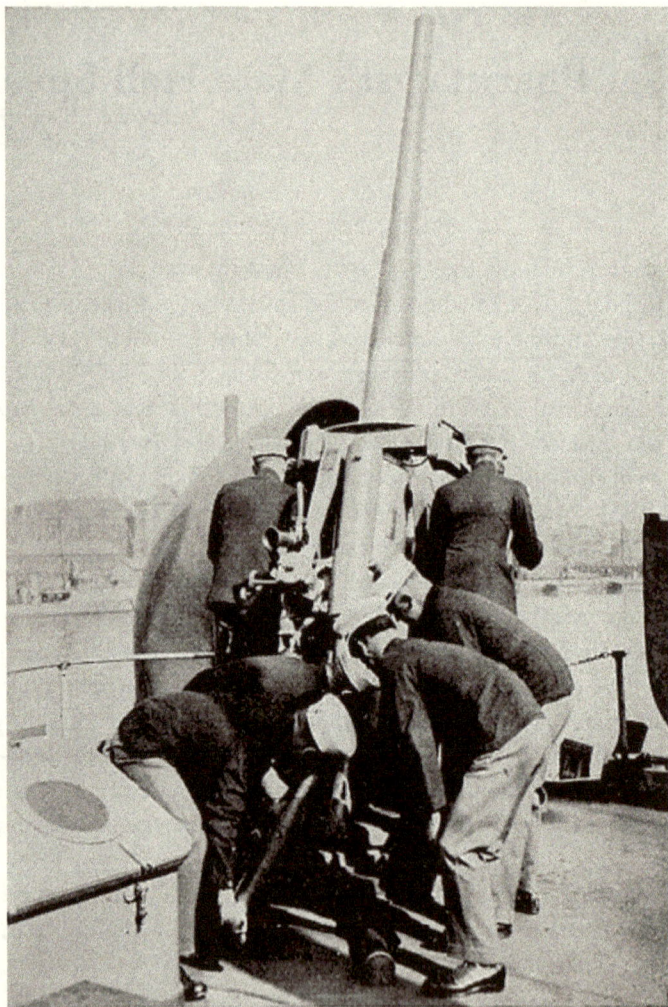

Marines on the job—manning the anti-aircraft guns.

was brought out strongly—we were in the service to save lives. Get that into your head! It was drummed into ours. We began to think we were privileged people because, while we were in the war, it just happened to be our job to save life instead of taking it.

I don't mean by that that we wouldn't relish a chance to get a crack at Fritz, the killer of women and babes, but our official task happened to be helping poor chaps back who had been laid low by a piece of Hun steel.

Once I had got my rating, I was told to report for duty on a destroyer. That just about suited me. I had been scared to death that they'd hold me at a base hospital, with no chance to cross the briny deep, and I went in search of my chum to say goodbye.

He was a quiet sort of chap, with a pair of horn-rimmed glasses that won for him the name of "Specs." He was as funny off duty as a goat, but the best corps man I have ever seen on his job. We were always together. We had plugged through the course together, and worried about the exams together, and we had hoped that fate would be kind to us and send us across on the same ship. But nothing doing. I parted from him with all kinds of promises to write and went aboard the destroyer.

The first man I saw on deck was "Specs," double glasses and all. I couldn't believe my eyes. I stared at him like a fool. And by crikey, it turned out to be his brother, who was coxswain and enough like "Specs" to pass for himself. Well, needless to say, Trace and I hit it up from the word go.

We had a few accident cases which kept me fairly busy going over, but as we came nearer the Zone I got the fever that runs in every man's blood to catch a sight of Fritz. There were some fellows aboard who had crossed a half-dozen times without a squint at a submarine and with nothing fiercer to take a shot at than a sleepy whale.

We were escorting a merchant ship flotilla—a whole flock of us. It had been an exciting day all right! Early that morning, while it was yet dark, we had made out what seemed to us to be a ring of little lights upon the water. Take it from me, we don't rush in on anything like that. It may be a German's coy trap for blowing you sky high. But we sure were curious and we circled the lights swiftly, by no means certain but that every minute would be our last. As we approached them we made them out. They were lifeboats full of men signalling wildly for help.

We flew to their rescue and picked them up. The lot of them were half frozen and barely able to tell us the old story of Fritz's stab in the dark. I had some work to do then! There were frostbitten hands and feet and ears to care for, and chills and fever to ward off. I worked over them for hours. We found out that they were the crew of a British cargo ship and as soon as it was light we landed them at a nearby port and set out to sea again.

It was a wild morning. The wind had risen to what was fast becoming a gale. Think of a gale at sea in November! Icy waves sweep your deck and toss your ship about like a ball in the water. No chance to cook a mouthful, as nothing would stay on the range long enough—hardtack for all hands and lucky to get it—stand by as best you can in case of a lurking Fritz.

The gale grew worse. I had never seen such an ugly storm. The sky was almost black and the sea was running so high that it seemed as though green mountains were crashing down upon us as the combers fell. I don't know how we happened to weather it, but once the wind died down, we saw some distance away a British destroyer, bobbing about aimlessly on that wild sea. Her decks had been swept clean, her propellers smashed, her wireless gone. She was just a plaything of the waves. We went to her rescue. What was left of her crew was certainly glad to see us. They had given up all hope of help coming before Fritz saw her.

We towed her to her base and on the way we caught a signal warning us to keep an extra sharp lookout as a cruiser had been sent to bottom by a submarine not five miles away. We left the disabled destroyer at her base and set out for our own; it was about four in the afternoon. The storm had died down, but the waves still looked wicked and the sky was a dirty gray.

Fritz was laying for us. I suppose he had seen us taking the destroyer in and he figured we'd start for home. I guess he decided to make a good day's work of it by sinking us before he sat down to dinner. Trace was lookout, and he sighted a small periscope some distance off the port bow. It extended about a foot out of water and was visible only a few seconds, but say, did he let out a yell? . . .

We charged them. Three seconds later we dropped a depth charge. That's quick work for you. Hot on her trail we were and no mistake! Another destroyer speeded up too and followed the spray that told which way Fritz was heading. Oh, he was still determined to get one of us, for he was making straight for a merchant vessel in the convoy. We dropped another charge.

96

At that instant the submarine's conning tower appeared on the surface between ourselves and the convoy. Did we pump hell into her from our stern gun? We did!

Up came the bow of the submarine. She was down by the stern, but righted herself and seemed to increase her speed. We were after her like a streak. We fired from our bow gun. That settled Fritz. For, after the third shot, the crew of the submarine came on deck and surrendered, by God! to the U. S. N.!

The whole thing took exactly ten minutes, but it seemed a lifetime to me!

We approached the submarine to pick up the prisoners, while the other destroyers kept their batteries trained on the boat. We weren't taking any chances, for there's no telling if Fritz, with his hands up, won't pull a trigger with his toes.

We got a line to the submarine, but in a few moments she sank. The line was let go and the U-boat's crew jumped into the water and swam to our ship. All of them wore life preservers, but some of the men were exhausted when they reached the side of our ship, and, as the submarine sank, several of them were caught by the radio aerial and carried below the surface before they could disentangle themselves.

Ten of the men were so weak that we had to pass lines under their arms to haul them aboard, and one chap was in such a condition that he could not hold a line thrown him. I saw him reach for it and let it slip through his fingers. I couldn't stand it. I climbed the rail, and, before they could stop me, I dived in. Someone dived after me. It was Trace. He felt like I did seeing a man drown before your eyes. More credit was due him, though, by a long sight, than me, for his job was coxswain while I was in a corps that was supposed to save life. Fine corps man I'd have made if, at my first chance to rescue a fellow, I'd stood by and let him go down!

We were hauled aboard with the German between us. I've never been so cold in my life. I bet you could hear my teeth chatter clear across the Atlantic. As for the German, he died in a few minutes' time. The reason is plain. I wasn't able to give him first aid, being all in myself. I know I could have pulled him through. Those other chaps were no good at resuscitation.

We had four German officers and a crew of thirty-five prisoners. The first lot taken in this war by an American destroyer.

We fed up Fritz on hot coffee and sandwiches. Our method of

handling prisoners is a bit different from the Huns. They were a pretty seedy lot, but once we had shelled out warm coats and heavy clothing to them, they perked up a bit and before long the crew began to sing. I listened to them, but somehow it made me sick. I had heard how they treat our men when they catch them—they don't get much chance to sing!

The German officers told us that the first depth charge had wrecked Fritz's machinery and caused him to sink to a considerable depth. If we did say so ourselves, we were pretty good shots!

There wasn't a mark on the submarine that gave her away, but the lifebelts did. We got her number. We proceeded to port and there turned our prisoners over under guard. We felt pretty cocky over it. Or rather the crew did who had had a real hand in capturing the Germans. I hadn't done anything. Why they mentioned me in the reports I don't know. I guess they didn't remember about a corps-man's job including the saving of life—I did, though. I told you I had studied hard!

Fireman Seymour Speaks

Fritz Gets Tagged

I belong to the Black Gang. You don't hear much about us because our work keeps us below deck, and it's good hard work when you're making twenty knots—but I like it. I wouldn't change places with any gun's crew on earth, although they have more of a chance for their life if trouble comes. We have duties to perform right in our quarters in case a ship is struck that keeps us close to the engines—there's always danger there—especially aboard a coal-burning destroyer—and that's what I shipped on.

There wasn't any keeping me out of the navy. We have four honourable discharges hung up in our house. I used to show them to my kid. He's five, but awful smart. He knows all about them.

"That's from the War of 1776," he'll say, pointing to the first one.

"And that's from the Civil War, my great Grandpa fought in that."

The third one is for the Spanish-American.

"My grandpa fought in that one," he tells you.

And pretty soon, when this scrap is over there'll be a fourth one hanging alongside of the others and Bill can look at it and say, "My pop got that one in the biggest war of all."

I only wish the youngster was old enough to enlist himself. We're a fighting family. I joined the navy in 1915. I was on a battleship then, but when war broke they transferred me to a destroyer. We didn't go out until the cold weather had set in. All of us were given Arctic outfits and it's lucky we were—we needed them, believe me! You are mighty grateful for the heavy woollen pants and the jumper with a hood that covers your ears.

Destroyer duty is the most exciting of all, for, while merchant crafts go out of their way to avoid submarines, our game is to go out of our way to hunt them. It was like a game of hide and seek, with a destroyer

"It," trying to tag Fritz if he'd only give us half a chance.

One of Fritz's pet stunts was to send us an S.O.S., giving us the exact location at sea of a vessel in trouble—oh, he was awful careful to see that you got it right, all you needed to do was to steam up to that spot and be blown clear out of creation.

Of course, all the calls for help weren't false. One day we came close enough to see a cargo ship in flames, and her crew being ordered over her side to open boats. "Burn the cargo and sink the ship," was Fritz's creed and if you think that being set afloat in a life-boat in December is an experience you'll forget in a hurry, you're wrong!

By the time we reached the survivors, half of them were dead—frozen where they sat, their bodies covered with ice.

We were on duty every minute of the day and night. I don't think any of the crew slept soundly for the seven months that we stayed at sea without ever touching shore. Think of it, seven months on a ship that's never still, zigzagging, doubling on its own course—charging any floating objects in hopes of downing a Fritz.

My, but the troopships were glad to see us when we went out to meet them. We'd shoot up alongside of them, or cut clean across their bow, playing in front of them like a porpoise, as we asked them what sort of a trip they had had across and how things were going back home. We'd come so close to the convoy at times that they could almost reach out and touch us, then we'd dart away at the drop of a hat.

As Christmas came near, we hoped to touch port. We had been promised a Christmas ashore, but it seemed we had sudden orders to go out and pick up a convoy, so we headed for the open sea again.

Christmas Eve was biting cold. I went up for air and I was glad to hurry back to the engine room again. It was at least warm down there. The men who stood watch on deck were muffled to the eyes. I thought of my wife and the kid. I wondered if he was hanging up his little stocking and saying a prayer for his dad who was at sea. I hadn't heard a word from them, of course, since I had left home. But on that particular night they seemed very close to me. I could almost see our little sitting room, with a holly wreath in the window. I remembered just the corner where we always put up the Christmas tree and I thought of the fun we had trimming it and trying not to make a breath of noise to wake the kid. All this while I realized dimly that the boat was pitching harder than ever and my mate broke in with:

"We're in for a gale to celebrate Christmas proper."

We were, all right! They say it was the worst storm that had been seen off that coast in many a year. It was the highest sea I've ever been on. You could scarcely keep your feet, and as for food—our Christmas dinner consisted of hard tack and lucky we were to get that. You couldn't keep a thing on the ranges except the stationary kettles. They managed to make something that was supposed to be coffee in those and for twenty-two hours that was our chow.

There were moments through that long night when I thought we'd turn clean over. We never expected the rudder to hold with those giant waves breaking over the deck and turning everything to ice.

All the submarines afloat didn't give me the feeling of nearness to death that that storm had. I certainly was glad when the sea quieted down and the sun struggled through the clouds again.

Up to the first of the year we had not had a chance to get a shot at Fritz. He had been a bit too wily for us, getting in his dirty work before we arrived on the spot, leaving a trail of burning or sinking ships but no sign of himself. But we got our revenge. It was in January. We had met a string of troop and cargo ships from the States, which we were escorting to port. We were so near the coast that I guess most of the boys aboard were getting their things together preparatory to landing.

It was eight o'clock in the morning and I don't suppose any of us really dreamed of a submarine turning up so close to shore, when suddenly the shrill whistle from a transport made the air around it blue with its noise! A second later came the roar of guns and I knew sure enough that some tin fish had welcomed us!

I stood by in the engine room, which was my place in time of danger, listening with all my ears to the boom of our own guns. Oh, we were after Fritz all right!

The rumor drifted in to us that there were ten periscopes to be seen, but soon it came down to three. The guns from all the ships thundered—it was as if a battlefield were transported to the Atlantic Ocean.

The roar of guns deafened you, but you certainly got a thrill you never forgot. We worked like fiends. We knew they needed speed as never before. We were like cats after a mouse.

Someone sent up a shout and word came that oil had begun to show on the water—that meant one less submarine afloat! Again the roar of guns—again the shout! Two Fritzes sunk. . . !

In the midst of the firing came a strange new sound—a buzzing overhead. French airships to the rescue! They were not more than two hundred yards above us, dropping bombs as they flew. I listened for the sound of cheering—it came! A third Fritz sunk. In port the sinking was officially verified—three German submarines destroyed, read the record. Not bad, eh?

I don't believe a gun on any of the transports or destroyers was cold for fully two hours. When it was over, I went on deck for a breath of air. I was sweating like a horse and shaking all over from the strain. The instant I stepped on deck, Fritz got a shot at us, splintering our deck and taking one of my fingers along as a souvenir.

Now I ask you, wasn't that rum luck? If I'd only stayed below where I belonged, I'd still be plus a finger. The ship's doctor finished up the job, but I couldn't use that hand, and, believe me, it made me sore as anything. I knew I'd miss all the sport going by having to be sent home. I tried to argue with him. But he wouldn't listen to me—home I must go. There wasn't any two ways about it—orders is orders.

I traveled back on a transport. I was all right. My hand was healing fine. I wanted to stand watch on the way across, but they wouldn't let me. Treated me like a blooming invalid and gave me a month's liberty to get well. Well! I was well ten minutes after it happened.

No, I didn't tell my wife how I lost it. I said I'd been mixed up in an accident in the engine room. That was pretty near the truth. You can slip so easily with the ship pitching and rearing that it isn't hard to lose an arm that way. Oh, if I was to tell her that a sub carried part of my hand away, she'd worry to death about having me go to sea again. I'll break it to her after the war. Just now there's one thing on my mind—just one—to get back somehow in the Black Gang. I can handle a shovel—my arm's a bit stiff yet, but I'm all muscle. Believe me, they aren't going to shelve me just because one finger's gone! Not by a long sight!

I'm not going to miss one minute of this scrap if I can help it. My kid's going to be proud of my record before I get through—wait and see if he isn't!

Warrant Carpenter Hoyt Speaks

THE FLOWER OF FRANCE

Ever see those red poppies that grow by the roadside in France? They always make me think of Angele. They are so graceful and vivid and gay. It almost seems as though they enjoyed watching the soldiers march past, they spring up so close to the road. All the war that has swept through the land has failed to kill the crop. You will find innumerable scarlet patches of them nodding their brave little heads to the boys as they tramp by—cheering them on—for all the world like France's daughters—bless them!

I was one of the first Americans to go across after our declaration of war on Germany. Those were the days when the German propagandists in this country knew more about the movements of our fleet than we did ourselves.

They called upon us formally a way off the French coast, with two torpedoes. But they were bad shots, so their visiting cards never arrived and we continued our course without any further opportunity of making their acquaintance.

As we neared the coast the water became clotted up with wreckage—boxes and barrels and floating planks—yes—and bodies, too. I've never seen a sight to equal it and I have crossed eight times all told. But in the beginning of the war Fritz was pretty active. Never a day passed that we received less than seven or eight S.O.S. calls. Oh, Fritz was having it all his own way then. We've changed all that—rather!

I'll never forget the little French port where we dropped anchor. Nothing I can ever see in the years to come—with the exception of the Allied flags floating over the *Kaiser's* palace in Berlin—will equal the thrill I got from watching the first khaki-clad Yankees marching up that narrow street to the tune of Yankee Doodle!

I kept wondering who the dickens I was, to be privileged to witness such a history-making sight!

The townsfolk mobbed us. They cheered us and hugged us and called down blessings on our heads. Someone took pity on us and showed us the way to an inn—a rambling white *shallet* with a big American flag hung from its windows. At the gate, the innkeeper and his plump little wife were awaiting us with open arms. They asked us if we would consent to eat *"poullet."* Consent! We would have devoured birch bark with a relish had it been cooked the way Madame Mousequet could cook!

I have never tasted such chicken or such potatoes. And while we ate and drank the little lady fluttered about us, hoping, in voluble French, that everything suited "the dear officers from the United States."

They would not take a cent of pay for the feast. It was, they assured us, *"une grande honneur."* Over and over they insisted that we must not think of spoiling their pleasure by having money pass between us. What can you do with people like that?

That night we went to a little cinema theatre. When the lights were turned up and the audience caught sight of us, they rose in a body and cheered us. In one of the boxes were a group of French officers and their wives. One of the officers hurried around to where we were sitting.

"You must place yourself where all the people may see you," he insisted. There was no refusing him. He was like a child, bubbling over with joy at having us there.

"Come," he pleaded, "let me seat you so that all may see."

We followed meekly. The ladies in the box were awaiting us eagerly. They welcomed us with outstretched hands. And as I looked at those people who had been through two grilling years of war, I thanked God I came from a country that had taken up arms against a beast who was trying to crush the red poppies beneath his heel.

It was hard to get leave to go up to Paris. Sailings were uncertain and special permission had to be obtained, but I made up my mind I'd go. General Pershing was to be there for the Fourth of July celebration at the tomb of Lafayette. I knew that would be a never-to-be-forgotten sight.

I was right. It was a glorious morning and the thrill of the day was in the air—crowds everywhere—sky blue and navy blue uniforms rubbing shoulders with the khaki of our own boys. Women, many of them in black, hurrying—hurrying toward the spot where the great Commander-in-Chief of the American Expeditionary Forces could be seen.

"Pershing!" Everywhere you heard his name and an under-current of eager whispers as to whether there would be a chance to see him or not.

The Fourth of July! Paris! And our general, the idol of the hour! I tell you it thrilled me clear down to my heels!

We navy men were let through the crowd and we were able to view the ceremony at close range. I have never heard such cheering in my life! It was Paris' first opportunity to hear our general speak, and he spoke so simply—so quietly—in the face of that great ovation that there was not one among us who could doubt his ability to lead our men as they had never before been led.

There were to be fireworks that night in honour of our presence— concerts and speeches and dancing. Oh, France was showing us that she was glad we had come, but how glad we were to be there she can never guess!

I drifted idly with the crowd. I wandered down to the big station—the *Gare de Lyons*. What took me there I scarcely know. Fate, I suppose, because there were a thousand and one places I might have gone instead.

The station was full of a bustling mob—uniforms—uniforms everywhere. A train load of soldiers had just arrived on leave from the Front. That was a sight for you, as their eager eyes lighted on some loved one's face! I tell you, it kept your heart jumping in your throat to see them. Some of them were so white and worn and haggard. Most of them bronzed and wiry, a bit grimy from the long train trip, with uniforms faded and sometimes torn. But weariness and dirt and tears could not hide the spirit that shone in their eyes as they clasped their wife and little ones to them.

A young artillery officer came toward me. He was a handsome man with a bit of a swagger in spite of his limp. I saw his eyes roving the crowd restlessly in search of someone. Suddenly he caught sight of me.

"Ah! An American! What joy! *Vive L'Amerique!*" he shouted.

I thanked him. I told him my name and he told me his. It was Louis du Frere, and he lived at Faubourg St. Germain. He was just back from the trenches on a precious leave of seven days. Wounded? He shrugged. But, yes, fifteen times so far, and what of that?

I stared at him. Wounded fifteen times and yet eager to go back! Spirit of France, you are indomitable!

He excused himself as he scanned the crowd. His sister was to meet him. She was there somewhere. She never failed him. Ah, yes! He had found her. . . .

I turned to see a little black-clad figure rush into his arms and cling to him as though she could never let him go. He spoke to her gently.

"Angele," he said, "this gentleman is a great officer of the American navy. Tell him how glad you are to welcome him to France."

At that she whirled and since then I have never been able to see a red poppy without thinking of her. I don't remember what I said in my very limited French, but her brother broke in to explain that she had lost her young husband at the Battle of the Marne and he ended up by announcing to her that I was going to spend the rest of my liberty as their guest.

I tried to protest, to insist that I had no intention of thrusting my presence upon them for eleven days. But he took my refusal with the air of a hurt child and when Angele joined her pleas with his, I succumbed. I let du Frere hail a cab and we all piled in. I gathered up my few possessions at the hotel and climbed aboard again, and we rumbled through the streets of Paris toward St. Germain, Angele clinging to her brother's arm and listening with a wrapt look on her face to his gay comments on trench life.

I thought I must be dreaming it all. It was so like the scene of a play—Paris slipping away from us, as we rattled across a long bridge, the open country becoming greener and leafier every instant—the gay voice of the young officer, the eager questions of our little old driver, and the poppy-like girl, with lips parted, drinking in breathlessly every word her brother uttered.

We stopped before a tiny house, shaded by tall trees. I saw, gathered before it, a little knot of people, shading their eyes for a glimpse of the returning hero.

They pounced upon him, men, women, and children—all his neighbours, who had awaited his home coming for heaven only knows how many hours. They shouted their welcome to him, each of them clasping him for a minute and claiming his full attention.

Angele stood looking on, the tears rolling down her cheeks, even while her lips smiled.

"They love him so," she said softly, as though to explain it, "he is so brave!"

I think he was, to face that mob.

They followed him in. The table was spread with every sort of delicacy. Each one of them had contributed something choice—some dish of which he was especially fond. He exclaimed over it all rapturously. He left nothing to be desired in his eager enthusiasm.

They gave him no time to rest. They poured a torrent of questions upon him. Questions about their own brothers and husbands and lovers—questions concerning warfare—trench life—battles in which he had fought. And he told them all he knew until at length Angele scolded them tenderly and bore him off. Then it was that they turned upon me as the second best object of interest.

Never in a lifetime could I answer all that they asked of me. What did our country hope to do? How many men could she send across at once? How long did she think the war would last?

I tell you I was glad to see Angele and Louis reappear and to follow them to the feast. I was placed at Angele's right hand—the guest of honour—I sat down with a sigh of relief as I saw the tempting spread. Sat down! We were never down more than an instant before someone would leap up and propose a standing toast to Pershing and to Joffre, to President Wilson and to President Poincairé, to myself, to my navy, to my country!

And the *Marseillaise!* How they did sing that! three and four times, shouting the chorus until the rafters shook!

Then Louis pounded on the table for order.

"The American officer will now sing his National Anthem," he announced.

There was instant silence, then encouraging applause, then silence.

"But yes, you will sing it," urged Angele, seeing my panic.

Now, in the first place, I cannot carry a tune and in the second place I knew just one verse of the "Star Spangled Banner"—and I was not over sure of that one!

I have never felt a shame equal to mine as I struggled desperately through the first verse of my country's song! They applauded madly. I might have been Caruso to judge from the racket they made.

But Louis was not satisfied.

"Permit me also to sing it for you," he said, and sing it he did—all three verses of it,—with a ring to his voice that thrilled me and held me spellbound. I asked him where he had learned it. It seems, he modestly explained, an American ambulance driver had employed his time in the trenches teaching it to him.

After supper we danced to the music of a string band. But Louis sat in a corner, surrounded by a group of older men and I could see they were in earnest, thrashing out the latest developments at the Front. That gave me a chance with Angele—or rather—half a chance, because her every thought was with her brother.

"He is all the world to me," she said.

She watched over him in spite of himself and when she concluded he must be tired, she whispered it to his friends and they began, one by one, to leave, in spite of his protests. He went with them to the door, shouting, waving, kissing his hand. When he came back to us he did look a bit done up.

"Ah, Angele, it is good to be at home," he said, and then, as though fearing that might seem a confession of weakness, he hastened to add, "for a little time!"

We spent six wonderfully lazy days in the heart of summer. It was there that I came to know the poppies which were so like Angele, so radiant, so graceful—so lovely. I told her once that she put me in mind of them.

"I am glad," she replied, "because I, too, love them."

My leave was not up for eleven days all told, and Louis had persuaded me to stay on at the little cottage after his return to duty. I did not need much persuading. It seemed as though I could never tear myself away from that tiny house shaded by tall trees.

The night before he left I don't think any of us slept a wink. The neighbours arrived, laden with all sorts of dainties—cakes and bread they had made for him to take back. They brought packages for their own boys, too, that he cheerfully promised to distribute. They gave him letters and a thousand messages, which he repeated painstakingly after them. He was so gentle with them, so eager to do as they asked.

He was particularly pleased over a little bunch of wild flowers a tiny girl had gathered for him, the flowers were drooping and faded from being clasped in her hot little hand, but he told her again and again how much he loved them, until her little cheeks glowed pink with joy and her eyes shone like stars.

After they had gone, I stole away and left Angele alone with him. They sat in the open doorway, her cheek against his arm, her hand in his. She was not sad, there was a happy, busy note in her voice as she chatted to him.

Before he climbed the stairs to bed, he sought me. I was smoking and thinking, on a little bench beneath the trees. Louis sat beside me and laid his hand on my knee.

"Well, my friend, I leave before you. For a little while we part, is it not so?—then, God willing, we meet again."

I tried to tell him what my visit had meant to me. What a place France and her people would forever more occupy in my heart. All those things I struggled to say, but when it comes to expressing that which lies close to our heart, I find we are a halting, tongue-tied nation!

Then I spoke of Angele. I wanted him to know before he left how much I cared for her. I was afraid he might be displeased, but, instead, he pumped my hand with joy.

"This is American fashion," he laughed, then he leaned over and kissed my cheek. "Since you love a French girl you will have to get used to her brother's greeting," he said.

I told him I had not spoken to Angele. I had not dared to. I could not hope she would care for me.

"But you must speak tonight, before I go," he shouted. "Let me prepare her first. Oh, but this is of a great happiness to me!"

And before I could stop him, he hurried away.

After a long silence, while my heart thumped against my ribs and I felt myself growing hot and cold by turns, his voice sounded through the darkness.

"Come here, my friend, and see what you can do to make this child change her mind."

I ran toward him. I saw the flash of Angele's white gown, but when I reached her side, Louis had gone. She awaited me. Somehow she looked like the poppies at twilight, when their petals are folded. . . .

We were there together so long, that at length Louis' voice broke in upon us and startled us. He shouted that he must leave in six hours—that a brother returning to the Front had some claim upon his sister's time. Angele flew to his side, begging him to forgive her selfishness, but he pinched her cheek and laughed at her, brimming over with happiness at the romance for which he claimed he was responsible.

"But you must not take her away until after the war," he pleaded. "I want her here to greet me when I come home. I am a selfish brute, I know, but I would have nothing to return to if my little sister were gone."

I promised him. I would have promised anything that night I was so happy. It did not seem, as I stood in that quiet, leafy garden, with Angele's hand in mine, that there could be pain and anguish in the world—that cannons could be roaring and star shells bursting less than a hundred miles away!

Louis left at daybreak. We drove to Paris with him and to the station. It was a gay morning with a red sun rolling up from the east.

Angele was all smiles and animation, full of eager plans for his next leave. She submitted to his teasing with a laugh, but, for all that, her eyes looked as though they held a world of unshed tears, and I saw her, once or twice, press her lips together as though to choke back the sobs.

The station was full of men returning to the Front. They called eagerly to one another—they compared packages, and boasted of the good times they had had. Louis caught my hand and wrung it. Then he laid Angele's in it.

"She is all I have," he said; "it is fitting I leave her in the care of our beloved ally."

He kissed her and teased her about capturing an American in seven days, saluted us smartly and stalked through the great gate, turning to wave and smile and kiss his hand.

I never felt such a sense of loss in my life. It seemed as though the sun had gone out of the day.

"I cannot bear it," Angele whispered, so I took her away.

We spent the few remaining days of my leave planning our life after the war. She will not marry me until then. She and Louis are coming to the States to live and we three are to be as happy as the days are long. We will be, too. I know it.

I have been across seven times since and I have seen her four of those times in the past year. If there is any man on earth who wants this war to end it is I—and the reason is a certain flower-like girl in France. Good Lord! you don't know what waiting for her means!

We've got to finish those Germans quickly and thoroughly so that Louis and Angele and I can set sail for America. If that is not a reason for ending this war, find me a better one!

LEONAUR

ALSO FROM LEONAUR
AVAILABLE IN SOFTCOVER OR HARDCOVER WITH DUST JACKET

BUGEAUD: A PACK WITH A BATON *by Thomas Robert Bugeaud*—The Early Campaigns of a Soldier of Napoleon's Army Who Would Become a Marshal of France.

WATERLOO RECOLLECTIONS *by Frederick Llewellyn*—Rare First Hand Accounts, Letters, Reports and Retellings from the Campaign of 1815.

SERGEANT NICOL *by Daniel Nicol*—The Experiences of a Gordon Highlander During the Napoleonic Wars in Egypt, the Peninsula and France.

THE JENA CAMPAIGN: 1806 *by F. N. Maude*—The Twin Battles of Jena & Auerstadt Between Napoleon's French and the Prussian Army.

PRIVATE O'NEIL *by Charles O'Neil*—The recollections of an Irish Rogue of H. M. 28th Regt.—The Slashers—during the Peninsula & Waterloo campaigns of the Napoleonic war.

ROYAL HIGHLANDER *by James Anton*—A soldier of H.M 42nd (Royal) Highlanders during the Peninsular, South of France & Waterloo Campaigns of the Napoleonic Wars.

CAPTAIN BLAZE *by Elzéar Blaze*—Life in Napoleons Army.

LEJEUNE VOLUME 1 *by Louis-François Lejeune*—The Napoleonic Wars through the Experiences of an Officer on Berthier's Staff.

LEJEUNE VOLUME 2 *by Louis-François Lejeune*—The Napoleonic Wars through the Experiences of an Officer on Berthier's Staff.

CAPTAIN COIGNET *by Jean-Roch Coignet*—A Soldier of Napoleon's Imperial Guard from the Italian Campaign to Russia and Waterloo.

FUSILIER COOPER *by John S. Cooper*—Experiences in the 7th (Royal) Fusiliers During the Peninsular Campaign of the Napoleonic Wars and the American Campaign to New Orleans.

FIGHTING NAPOLEON'S EMPIRE *by Joseph Anderson*—The Campaigns of a British Infantryman in Italy, Egypt, the Peninsular & the West Indies During the Napoleonic Wars.

CHASSEUR BARRES *by Jean-Baptiste Barres*—The experiences of a French Infantryman of the Imperial Guard at Austerlitz, Jena, Eylau, Friedland, in the Peninsular, Lutzen, Bautzen, Zinnwald and Hanau during the Napoleonic Wars.

LEONAUR

ALSO FROM LEONAUR
AVAILABLE IN SOFTCOVER OR HARDCOVER WITH DUST JACKET

THE LIFE OF THE REAL BRIGADIER GERARD VOLUME 1—THE YOUNG HUSSAR 1782-1807 *by Jean-Baptiste De Marbot*—A French Cavalryman Of the Napoleonic Wars at Marengo, Austerlitz, Jena, Eylau & Friedland.

THE LIFE OF THE REAL BRIGADIER GERARD VOLUME 2—IMPERIAL AIDE-DE-CAMP 1807-1811 *by Jean-Baptiste De Marbot*—A French Cavalryman of the Napoleonic Wars at Saragossa, Landshut, Eckmuhl, Ratisbon, Aspern-Essling, Wagram, Busaco & Torres Vedras.

THE LIFE OF THE REAL BRIGADIER GERARD VOLUME 3—COLONEL OF CHASSEURS 1811-1815 *by Jean-Baptiste De Marbot*—A French Cavalryman in the retreat from Moscow, Lutzen, Bautzen, Katzbach, Leipzig, Hanau & Waterloo.

THE INDIAN WAR OF 1864 *by Eugene Ware*—The Experiences of a Young Officer of the 7th Iowa Cavalry on the Western Frontier During the Civil War.

THE MARCH OF DESTINY *by Charles E. Young & V. Devinny*—Dangers of the Trail in 1865 by Charles E. Young & The Story of a Pioneer by V. Devinny, two Accounts of Early Emigrants to Colorado.

CROSSING THE PLAINS *by William Audley Maxwell*—A First Hand Narrative of the Early Pioneer Trail to California in 1857.

CHIEF OF SCOUTS *by William F. Drannan*—A Pilot to Emigrant and Government Trains, Across the Plains of the Western Frontier.

THIRTY-ONE YEARS ON THE PLAINS AND IN THE MOUNTAINS *by William F. Drannan*—William Drannan was born to be a pioneer, hunter, trapper and wagon train guide during the momentous days of the Great American West.

THE INDIAN WARS VOLUNTEER *by William Thompson*—Recollections of the Conflict Against the Snakes, Shoshone, Bannocks, Modocs and Other Native Tribes of the American North West.

THE 4TH TENNESSEE CAVALRY *by George B. Guild*—The Services of Smith's Regiment of Confederate Cavalry by One of its Officers.

COLONEL WORTHINGTON'S SHILOH *by T. Worthington*—The Tennessee Campaign, 1862, by an Officer of the Ohio Volunteers.

FOUR YEARS IN THE SADDLE *by W. L. Curry*—The History of the First Regiment Ohio Volunteer Cavalry in the American Civil War.

LEONAUR

ALSO FROM LEONAUR
AVAILABLE IN SOFTCOVER OR HARDCOVER WITH DUST JACKET

LIFE IN THE ARMY OF NORTHERN VIRGINIA *by Carlton McCarthy*— The Observations of a Confederate Artilleryman of Cutshaw's Battalion During the American Civil War 1861-1865.

HISTORY OF THE CAVALRY OF THE ARMY OF THE POTOMAC *by Charles D. Rhodes*—Including Pope's Army of Virginia and the Cavalry Operations in West Virginia During the American Civil War.

CAMP-FIRE AND COTTON-FIELD *by Thomas W. Knox*—A New York Herald Correspondent's View of the American Civil War.

SERGEANT STILLWELL *by Leander Stillwell* —The Experiences of a Union Army Soldier of the 61st Illinois Infantry During the American Civil War.

STONEWALL'S CANNONEER *by Edward A. Moore*—Experiences with the Rockbridge Artillery, Confederate Army of Northern Virginia, During the American Civil War.

THE SIXTH CORPS *by George Stevens*—The Army of the Potomac, Union Army, During the American Civil War.

THE RAILROAD RAIDERS *by William Pittenger*—An Ohio Volunteers Recollections of the Andrews Raid to Disrupt the Confederate Railroad in Georgia During the American Civil War.

CITIZEN SOLDIER *by John Beatty*—An Account of the American Civil War by a Union Infantry Officer of Ohio Volunteers Who Became a Brigadier General.

COX: PERSONAL RECOLLECTIONS OF THE CIVIL WAR--VOLUME 1 *by Jacob Dolson Cox*—West Virginia, Kanawha Valley, Gauley Bridge, Cotton Mountain, South Mountain, Antietam, the Morgan Raid & the East Tennessee Campaign.

COX: PERSONAL RECOLLECTIONS OF THE CIVIL WAR--VOLUME 2 *by Jacob Dolson Cox*—Siege of Knoxville, East Tennessee, Atlanta Campaign, the Nashville Campaign & the North Carolina Campaign.

KERSHAW'S BRIGADE VOLUME 1 *by D. Augustus Dickert*—Manassas, Seven Pines, Sharpsburg (Antietam), Fredericksburg, Chancellorsville, Gettysburg, Chickamauga, Chattanooga, Fort Sanders & Bean Station.

KERSHAW'S BRIGADE VOLUME 2 *by D. Augustus Dickert*—At the wilderness, Cold Harbour, Petersburg, The Shenandoah Valley and Cedar Creek..

LEONAUR

ALSO FROM LEONAUR
AVAILABLE IN SOFTCOVER OR HARDCOVER WITH DUST JACKET

THE 9TH—THE KING'S (LIVERPOOL REGIMENT) IN THE GREAT WAR 1914 - 1918 *by Enos H. G. Roberts*—Mersey to mud—war and Liverpool men.

THE GAMBARDIER *by Mark Severn*—The experiences of a battery of Heavy artillery on the Western Front during the First World War.

FROM MESSINES TO THIRD YPRES *by Thomas Floyd*—A personal account of the First World War on the Western front by a 2/5th Lancashire Fusilier.

THE IRISH GUARDS IN THE GREAT WAR - VOLUME 1 *by Rudyard Kipling*—Edited and Compiled from Their Diaries and Papers—The First Battalion.

THE IRISH GUARDS IN THE GREAT WAR - VOLUME 1 *by Rudyard Kipling*—Edited and Compiled from Their Diaries and Papers—The Second Battalion.

ARMOURED CARS IN EDEN *by K. Roosevelt*—An American President's son serving in Rolls Royce armoured cars with the British in Mesopatamia & with the American Artillery in France during the First World War.

CHASSEUR OF 1914 *by Marcel Dupont*—Experiences of the twilight of the French Light Cavalry by a young officer during the early battles of the great war in Europe.

TROOP HORSE & TRENCH *by R.A. Lloyd*—The experiences of a British Life-guardsman of the household cavalry fighting on the western front during the First World War 1914-18.

THE EAST AFRICAN MOUNTED RIFLES *by C.J. Wilson*—Experiences of the campaign in the East African bush during the First World War.

THE LONG PATROL *by George Berrie*—A Novel of Light Horsemen from Gallipoli to the Palestine campaign of the First World War.

THE FIGHTING CAMELIERS *by Frank Reid*—The exploits of the Imperial Camel Corps in the desert and Palestine campaigns of the First World War.

STEEL CHARIOTS IN THE DESERT *by S. C. Rolls*—The first world war experiences of a Rolls Royce armoured car driver with the Duke of Westminster in Libya and in Arabia with T.E. Lawrence.

WITH THE IMPERIAL CAMEL CORPS IN THE GREAT WAR *by Geoffrey Inchbald*—The story of a serving officer with the British 2nd battalion against the Senussi and during the Palestine campaign.

9 781782 820932